Private Equity Finance Made Easy

Step-by-Step Private Equity Finance, Fundraising, Valuation & PE Deals Guide for Startup Founders, Entrepreneurs, Fund Managers & Investment Bankers

UMRAN NAYANI

© *2023 UMRAN NAYANI | **ONECALL** Business Solutions*

© Copyright 2023 Umran Nayani | All Rights Reserved | Copyright Protected with www.ProtectMyWork.com | Reference Number: 15755031023S079

Second Edition: Restructured and Re-formatted to enhance the quality of your reading experience.

All intellectual property rights are reserved. Without written permission from the publisher, no part of this publication may be duplicated in any form or by any means, electronic or mechanical, including photocopying, recording, or any information browsing, storing, or retrieval system.

The publisher and author accept no responsibility for any errors, inaccuracies, omissions, or other inconsistencies in this publication. However, it is aimed to give accurate information on the subject matter discussed.

This publication is intended to provide readers with helpful information, but it is not meant to substitute direct expert guidance. A qualified professional should be contacted if this level of assistance is required. Unless otherwise stated, all of the characters and events in this book are fictional.

Note to My Readers: Every attempt has been made to simplify the sophisticated realm of Private Equity. If anything comes up that seems too complicated, write me an email umran@onecallbusinesssolutions.com, and I will work with you to explain it in simpler terms.

If you have any questions or feedback regarding the content and quality of your reading experience (*including but not limited to an inadvertent grammatical error or an editing issue*), please email me at umran@onecallbusinesssolutions.com. I promise to fix any of the highlighted points to your satisfaction.

PS *I respond to all my emails personally and take feedback from my readers very seriously.*

Table of Content

Section 1: Introduction and Overview of Private Equity 7

   1. Introduction and Welcome to Private Equity Finance Made Easy 7

   2. An Overview of Private Equity Investing 9

   3. The Benefits and Drawbacks of VC and PE Funding 10

Section 2: How Do Private Equity Funds Work? 11

   4. How to Set Up a Private Equity Fund 11

   5. The Structure of a Private Equity Fund: What You Need to Know 14

   6. Private Equity Fund Partnerships: Limited Partnerships 16

   7. Roles in a Private Equity Fund 18

   8. Understanding Management Buyout and its Intricacies 19

   9. What is a Leveraged Buyout, and what does it involve? 21

   10. Dispelling the Management Buyout (MBO) Myths 22

   11. Glossary of Investors 24

   12. Glossary of Buyout Terms 26

   13. Glossary of Investment Terms 28

   14. What is a Fund of Funds? 30

Section 3: The Characteristics of Private Equity Firms That Must Be Recognized 32

   15. Categorizing Private Equity Firms 32

   16. The Differences between Private Equity & Venture Capital Deal Stages 35

   17. A Private Equity Firm's Life Cycle 36

   18. How Do Private Equity Firms Create Value? 38

   19. The Measurement of Private Equity and Compensation 40

Section 4: The Right Private Equity Firm to Work With 42

   20. How to Find Investor-Deal Fit 42

   21. Is Private Equity the Best Alternative for Your Firm? 44

   22. Checklist for Selecting a Private Equity Fund 46

Section 5: How Do Private Equity Firms Find Deals? 48

23. Funding Transactions in Venture Capital and Private Equity: What They Are and How They Work 48
24. What Features Should a Potential Buyout Target Have? 50
25. Screening for Private Equity Transactions 52
26. Funnel for Investing in Private Equity 54

Section 6: Deal Structuring for Private Equity Funds 55

27. Capital Structure of a Private Equity Acquisition 55
28. What are Equity and Common Stock, and what do they represent? 57
29. Preferred Stock in Private Equity Transactions 61
30. Preference Paid to Preferred Stockholders on Liquidation of the Company .. 63
31. More Rights for Private Equity Investors 64
32. Examining Capital Structures in Private Equity Transactions 66

Section 7: Value Creation and Metrics 68

33. How Do Private Equity Firms Make Money? 68
34. How Do PE Firms Generate Value for a Portfolio Company? 73

Section 8: The Deal Process in Private Equity 75

35. The Deal Process in a Nutshell - Part 1 75
36. The Deal Process in Private Equity - Part 2 77
37. Private Equity Deal Process - Part 3 79
38. Private Equity Deal Process - Part 4 80
39. Private Equity Deal Process - Part 5 81

Section 9: Private Equity Deal Due Diligence Processes 82

40. Private Equity Deal Due Diligence Processes 82
41. Competition and Markets - Competitive Due Diligence 82
42. Sector Expansion - Large Corporations Undergoing Commercial Due Diligence 84
43. Commercial Due Diligence - Customers and Suppliers 85
44. Commercial Due Diligence - Capital Requirements 87
45. Commercial Due Diligence - Financial Performance 87
46. Due Diligence in Financials 89

47. Legal Research - Legal Due Diligence 90

Section 10: Valuation and Pricing in Transactions 91

48. How Do I Value a Private Company in a Private Equity Deal? 91
49. What is EBITDA? 93

Section 11: Risks and Returns in Private Equity Investing 94

50. How to Assess Risk in Private Equity Investments 94
51. Equity in Leveraged Buyouts 95

Section 12: What Are the Exit Options When It Comes to Private Equity Transactions? 98

52. What is the Motivation for Taking on an LBO? 98
53. LBO Exit Options 100
54. What is Recapitalization? 101

Section 13: Trade Sales with M&A 102

55. Company Sales in LBO Exits 102
56. The Different Types of M&A Transaction Structures 103
57. Learning More about M&A Issues 105

Section 14: IPOs - Initial Public Offerings 106

58. LBO Exits: Initial Public Offerings 106
59. LBO Exits: IPO Process 107
60. Pros and Cons of an LBO Exiting an IPO 110

Section 15: Why Startups Fail? 113

61. Why Do Startups Fail? 113
62. Why Do Startups Fail? Pre-Investment Strategic Issues 114
63. Why Do Startups Fail? External Problems (Post-Investment Issues) 117
64. Why Do Startups Fail? (Internal Operational Problems) 119
65. Why Do Startups Fail? What Are the Most Common Key Management Issues? 121
66. Why Do Startups Fail? Finance Problems 123

Section 16: Fund Performance of Private Equity Funds 125

67. How Do I Go About Evaluating Private Equity Fund Performance? 125

68. What is the ROI of Private Equity Funds? 127

69. Defining Private Equity Fund Returns: What Do They Mean? 129

70. Return Ratios for Private Equity Funds 130

Section 17: Summary and Wrap-Up! *133*

71. Time to wrap up the Book and Summarize It. 133

72. Corporate Finance Further Learning 135

Section 1: Introduction and Overview of Private Equity

1. Introduction and Welcome to Private Equity Finance Made Easy

Private Equity Finance Made Easy is designed to assist you in learning more about PE Firms and how they operate. You'll find it extremely useful when you decide to take a Plunge into the World of opportunity within Private Equity. <u>Private Equity is an Asset Class, much like Publicly Traded Shares, Fixed-Income Bonds, or Real Estate.</u> Within the asset class of Private Equity, you may find Venture Capital Investment (Although fundamentals of Venture Capital and Private Equity are Polar Opposites), Equity Buyouts, and Distressed Debt.

As you will discover in this book, Private Equity firms employ various specialized investment techniques to subdivide the Private Equity asset class. Private Equity can be used in multiple ways, such as a Leveraged Buyout (LBO) or a Management Buyout (MBO). Venture Capital investment is generally considered a component of the asset class. It isn't a Private Equity investment. They're distinct assets in their own right and governed very differently. <u>When discussing "Private Equity," we discuss firms that organize and finance buyouts.</u> Private Equity is a complex topic. It's fascinating, but it's a unique ecosystem I'm excited about, and I can't wait to dive in deeper with you.

This book is written to give you a complete picture of the Private Equity ecosystem, from locating potential borrowers to monitoring their progress and closing their deals. You'll come away from it with much specific knowledge you won't have had before. I've given you a comprehensive and organized explanation of Private Equity financing in its broadest sense.

This book is well organized and has a logical sequence, and I hope you'll follow through. If you're a financial specialist, if you want to work in Private Equity, or are an entrepreneur who wants to learn more about this asset class to fund your business in the future, this book is for you. Let me summarize the major sections of this book, which have been considerably expanded and enhanced since I initially launched it. Section 1 is the book introduction and overview. In Section 2, we'll go through how Private Equity funds are structured and how they operate. We'll look at roles within Private Equity and what they signify.

The terminology in Private Equity is complex. The words may be tough to comprehend at times. The Glossary of Terms and Definitions in Section 3 is designed to help you break through the jargon.

We will also do a deep dive into the most significant features of Private Equity businesses. The life cycle, the phases, and characterizations are all topics covered in this book. There's much information on what Private Equity firms are made of. We'll look at how you, as an entrepreneur, can locate the best Private Equity firm for your company. We then learn how Private Equity firms discover their deals and the structure of Private Equity transactions. What is "Equity," and how does it differ from "Common Stock" and the nuts and bolts of a Private Equity Deal Structure? We will analyze a typical Private Equity transaction's Deal Value Creation and metrics.

Due Diligence is an essential element of the deal process, which is why I have devoted an entire section to it. We will learn how valuation and pricing are addressed in deals and the importance of the EBITDA. LBO modeling was unquestionably the most challenging aspect for me to develop. As you will discover, it's the longest Section in the book, but it doesn't teach you how to construct Excel formulas. It's about giving you a better understanding of an LBO model's underlying framework and structure and how everything fits together. We then move on to the risks and returns in Private Equity, which is undoubtedly critical. We'll look at the various exit options available in Private Equity transactions and recapitalizations. We'll look at trade sales as part of an M&A deal, followed by Initial Public Offerings (IPO), a typical exit mechanism for PE firms. We go through what they mean for investors and the companies themselves.

I will discuss the reasons for Startup failure with you at the end of the book. It's a helpful discussion for company CEOs and founders as they attempt to develop and finance their enterprises. We conclude the book by examining how you calculate returns to Private Equity Investors, General Partners, and Limited Partners in your operations. This is a very specialized topic that isn't particularly difficult but a specialist's area. It, therefore, has its Section.

As you can see, this is a comprehensive. Yet, it is a logically structured book where I'm sharing almost a decade of my Investment Banking study and Entrepreneurial experience with you. This is something I genuinely enjoy. And I hope that you get a lot from it.

If you have any questions or feedback regarding the content and quality of your reading experience, please write to me umran@onecallbusinesssolutions.com. I respond to all my emails personally and take input from my readers very seriously. Thank you for choosing "Private Equity Finance Made Easy." Let's dive in.

2. An Overview of Private Equity Investing

A Private Equity fund is a firm that invests in and takes control of a Company with the goal of boosting its Profits or Value by providing Capital and Expertise and then Selling the Stake at a Profit. The profit is eventually shared with those who have invested in the fund. A Private Equity fund is a type of mutual fund, and the investors are primarily **Institutional Investors** such as **Life Insurance Companies and Superannuation funds**. Private Equity funds invest in Non-public, Unlisted firms. (Since PE firms invest in "Equity," i.e., an investment in "Shares" rather than "Property" or "Financial instruments," and the Companies are privately held, the name "Private Equity" is coined).

Managers are usually paid based on an "**Investment management agreement.**" This is subject to the terms of the "**Trust deed**" that creates the fund and gets a return from the fund. The "**Fee**" is often referred to as a "**Performance fee**" and is based on how far above or below investment targets have returns been achieved by the fund. The fund manager decides whether or not to invest after obtaining approval from the investment committee.

Companies of all sizes utilize Private Equity financing to acquire and finance businesses, often known as Venture Capital Expansion, Capital Management Buyouts, and Public-to-Private transactions.

The Private Equity firm will buy shares in the company directly if it is looking to expand or develop cash. In a Management Buyout, the Private Equity firm will typically collaborate with two or three of the current senior executives of the target firm. The fund will generally invest 95 percent, with the management team investing 5 percent of the Equity. The acquirer will then purchase the target firm. To improve the potential profit for investors, most transactions are completed with borrowed funds and Private Equity investment money. Transactions are typically leveraged (i.e., financed with loans taken out under the firm name) to its maximum debt ceiling. A bank's senior debt will supply the majority of the borrowed funds. A second financier may provide further loans, known as mezzanine or junior debt. Subordinated debt, which ranks below all other loan funds, may also be convertible into Equity, for example, through a convertible loan note on the occurrence of certain events.

An "Exit" is a transaction in which a Private Equity firm "Sells" its investment. The business is often sold to a third-party buyer or floated on the stock market through an IPO with a share buyback. An IPO is the sale of stock to investors under a prospectus, allowing them to buy company shares. Some or all of the money raised is then used to acquire back the shares owned by the Private Equity firm. The average lifespan of a Private Equity fund is Ten years. This implies that the fund's investments are cyclical. The first set of investments follows the fund's establishment, and several exits occur three or four years later. **Secondary buyouts** are another trade, and many transactions are secondary purchases, which is when **one fund acquires the shares of another.**

3. The Benefits and Drawbacks of VC and PE Funding

Let's spend a few moments discussing the benefits and drawbacks of Venture Capital and Private Equity funding. We must examine these concerns. You must know what you're getting into if you deal with Venture Capitalists or Private Equity firms.

Advantages: They undoubtedly provide an excellent funding source, and capital is the lifeblood of any growing business. Because banks are typically risk-averse and don't like lending to high-growth or risky enterprises, it's extremely tough to come up with the required capital before the IPO phase or even acquire a trade investor. PE firms also fill a genuine gap in the market as a result of their experience. They also provide a wealth of sector knowledge and expertise. You've probably heard that the people who run Private Equity and Venture Capital firms have been doing it for a long time. They know how to invest in industries they understand and are familiar with. They can help you determine what you need to know and how to do it. They can also offer their expertise and knowledge to assist you.

Of course, they have extensive networks and connections to help you get excellent individuals like board advisors, a chairperson, or anything at the top of your company. But the most critical aspect is that they are willing to take risks. They take a far more optimistic approach to portfolios than most investors, believing that some businesses will fail while others will flourish.

As a result, it's worth investing. Hence, they are ready to take on the inherent danger of investing in an early-stage company (VC) or Growth Stage (PE). They're willing to invest, at least, a medium-term time horizon in the project. They don't demand their money back in six months, nine months, or a year. Now, let's look at the Disadvantages, shall we?

Disadvantages: The inability to exercise control and management autonomy. They're approaching to negotiate a contract insulating themselves from risk. This will be reflected in all the documentation, including the transaction paperwork and the shareholder agreement, which regulates your business relationship with investors after closing the deal.

So you can anticipate them to have many vetoes. They'll be able to fire you, among other things. You have typically given up complete management of your company to these investors. The investment process is lengthy and complex, requiring multiple steps and touch points. We're talking, at most, six months for a program and investment from beginning to end. And, of course, you should double-check that you have adequate cash for nine months or 12 months because there's no assurance that this deal will be completed, and there's a lot to it.

In most cases, the odds of closing the transaction are never in your favor. Going through this book, you'll better understand Venture Capital and Private Equity investment's intricacy. They may walk at any time unless they have a certain amount of money invested in the transaction. It's a gamble that is hard to evaluate. There's no assurance you'll receive the cash. There is a shift in risk from them to you. They'll ensure they're insulated by everything from their debt's seniority to their capacity to sack the board members and institute substantial changes to the company. You must realize that you're entering into a situation with a very bright, complex, and sophisticated investor. As a result, the relationship will reflect that degree of complexity. *If you're an entrepreneur, I don't want to scare you away from them, but I want to* **make sure that you've thought about your risk and the potential return.**

Section 2: How Do Private Equity Funds Work?

4. How to Set Up a Private Equity Fund

Let's suppose that you want to set up a Private Equity fund. This isn't the book's focus, and I'm not asking you to start your own fund. Of course, if that's something you're thinking about, good luck. However, creating a PE fund raises several intriguing concerns to help you comprehend how Private Equity works. To begin with, if you're establishing a fund, you must first determine **how to distinguish yourself in the market.** There are several vital pointers to consider. I won't get into specifics since much of it will be discussed in later chapters. However, you should have a **Sector focus**. Being a general fund won't cut it, especially if you're a new fund.

- What are your plans for the fund?
- What approach do you intend to take?
- What kind of investments will you make in the fund regarding the firm's lifecycle?
- How early in the firm's lifecycle are you going to be?
- Are you planning on creating a series fund?
- Is there a stage in the business's life cycle where you'll focus on "Development" or "Expansion"? There is much strategic foresight to be considered here.
- What sorts of geographic restrictions will you impose on yourself? There's a certain amount of practicality to be had there, too, because you don't want to be jetting all over the World when things aren't going so well.
- What sort of deals are you planning to make?
- Are you going to do Management Buyout deals?
- Are you going to do Leveraged Buyout deals?

There are a multitude of factors to consider. And, of course, what kind of investment amount are you planning to tackle? This is all related to your fund in some way. If your fund is worth $100 million, consider having 10-15 investments in the fund, which implies between five and ten million dollars per purchase. These are some of the critical choices you'll need to make about how you want to position yourself in the market. Once you have the basics in place, all that's left is to sit down and construct a business plan. You'll have to communicate this knowledge, and it'll have to be very well planned. Is this your first fund? In this scenario, your Business Plan will have to be impeccable.

If you have a track record, you'll still need the strategy for how your fund will differ. You'll likely establish a ten-year fund since that's the longest period you can guarantee investors. It is highly unusual, if not unheard of, for a first-time fund to have an evergreen fund and for you to need to establish a goal for how big the fund should be. That's also offset by your track record and how you'll expand. How are you going to use your first fund to grow this company? You must consider several aspects of your plan ahead of time and begin considering the types of investors you'll be courting.

Do you have a network you can contact directly, and they'll know your name? Then, you'll need to choose your attorneys' accountants. You call them lawyers in the UK. In the US, you called attorneys. Will you require any industry-specific knowledge to assist with your market definition? Another factor to consider is whether you'll need an Advisory board. An Advisory board consists of people with much expertise, particularly in the business and operational areas. An Advisory board can assist you in making decisions, especially about investments and company management. Then, after that, you must consider establishing your own business, which implies you'll have to come up with a name. It might include the strategy or not, so it may be a growth fund, or you might have a fund prepared. Consider using part of the technique's name. Alternatively, keep it clean to have multiple strategic options in the future. You'll almost certainly need to form a Limited Partnership or a Limited Liability Company (LLC). It would help if you began thinking more granularly about who will do what within the company.

Who are the Partners? The Partners are the top management of the company. You'll also need a CFO and a board member. **What are the different levels of employment that you'll have?** Then there's the executive structure beneath that. Directors, Assistant Directors, and Executives are all included in this group. People will be performing real transactions. **What is going to be your hiring strategy?** Who are you anticipating will join the team, or who do you expect you'll need to recruit?

It would be best to detail the organization's functions, such as **Deal Inception, Portfolio Management, Fundraising**, and, most importantly, **Compliance.** You'll need to establish your operation physically, so you'll have to find offices and install the necessary infrastructure. Acquire technology and set up any support personnel you'll require: secretaries. Consider your compensation structure, salaries, bonuses, profit sharing, health insurance, and retirement plans, which are all important for a company in fundraising. You'll start thinking about your private placement memorandum, your limited partner agreements with your investors, and the articles of association for your corporation. You'll have to consider your fee structure and management fees if you're going to charge them. These fees are deducted from the money destined for the fund, generally two percent each year. Then, you have to consider the carried interest rate. And will your carried interest kick in only after an anticipated hurdle rate of return, 5% or 8%? So, the Limited Partners receive a return before your carried interest return comes in.

Now it's time to get started fundraising. So far, you've done quite well, but you'll need an offering memorandum to offer to Limited Partners. They'll have to sign a subscription agreement when you tell them how much and how many shares they will purchase. You'll need a partnership agreement. A custodial agreement is required. You'll need due diligence research completed on you and the preparation of any marketing materials. When marketing, you must consider where you'll be going and who you'll approach to succeed.

Are you going on a tour? You'll be visiting various locations to meet with investors from other businesses. How will you demonstrate your track record of important queries, and how will you invest in your fund? The General Partners may invest less money in new funds, perhaps one or two percent. But if you've been there before and you have some money in the bank, they'll want to see more dedication. It could be around a two or three-percent requirement. Who is going to invest in your fund? Due to regulatory restrictions, It'll primarily be institutional and accredited investors in the US. These are, for example, insurance companies, national wealth funds, financial firms, pension funds, and university endowment funds. These are the kinds of individuals you'll be targeting to attract to your fund. When your fund has been established and is near to being closed, it will go through a first closing, then a final closing. It's time to put your cash to work. Congratulations! But you've only just begun the complicated work.

That's a brief rundown of how you may set up a Private Equity fund. As you can see, it requires structure. It must have several contracts in place. It must have a corporate entity. It would help if you had the appropriate personnel in place. You'll need a plan. There's a lot to consider. These are just some things to consider while researching investment funds, evaluating them, and looking at Private Equity funds. They're all critical topics to consider when examining market funds. That is a quick overview of how to establish a Private Equity fund. However, it has enough substance to provide you with some valuable nuggets of information that you may apply toward developing your Private Equity fund sector expertise.

5. The Structure of a Private Equity Fund: What You Need to Know

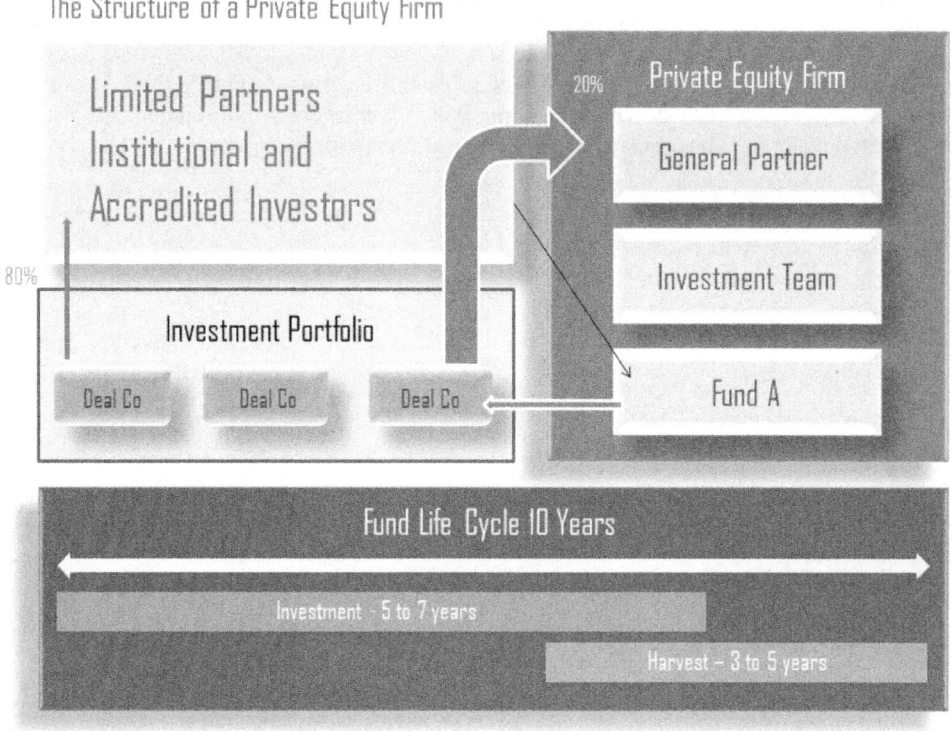

Let's take a closer look at the structure of a Private Equity firm. We will focus on the company's operational structure to better understand the link between "Limited Partners," i.e., the Investors, and the Private Equity Company, referred to as the "General Partner." The Limited Partners are the external investors who invest in the partnership. The leading partner is a Private Equity Company, which invests money for a return on its investment (usually 20% or higher). Limited Partners are often institutional or accredited investors. The laws don't specify what sorts of investors are permitted to invest. However, they must be sophisticated investors. Retail investors are not allowed to invest.

Alternative asset classes, such as Private Equity and Hedge funds, are used to achieve higher returns. They aim to obtain rates that exceed the S&P 500's by investing in non-traditional asset classes like Private Equity. This is part of their portfolio investment strategy. General Partners make a General Partner dedication, a promise to the fund. This cash belongs to the company, committed by the General Partners. It's generally in the one percent range, but it will be a substantial amount of their money.

Senior members of the Private Equity Company pledge, but it may also be open to executives at lower levels. The purpose is to ensure that the General Partners and Private Equity firm executives making critical investment decisions have skin in the game and that their interests are more closely aligned with institutional investors. It's also vital that this is a cash payout rather than a waiver of management fees or some other indirect investment approach. The General Partner invests the fund's cash into businesses, manages the portfolio, and then seeks to generate high returns through Exits. A typical Private Equity fund lasts ten years. According to industry sources, it takes approximately five to seven years for an investment to mature and be harvested. A fund's goal is to invest around 90% of its assets in the portfolio companies and keep a little bit back (typically 10%) for further investment into those firms for bolt-on acquisitions and growth capital.

A fund will have its own set of investment criteria. However, different funds within a firm might have other goals and objectives. New funds are raised to support the company's growth as existing reserves approach maturity and the total investment is achieved. This is a loop operation. Finally, a team inside the Private Equity Company is in charge of continuing and keeping the connections for the fund's growth while raising the following fund. Once they've finished a fund, the next one begins. The funds are typically closed over three years, and management fees are usually two percent per year on committed capital. For Limited Partners, there is a 20% carried interest above a minimum hurdle rate for the first several years after closing (3-5%). The Limited Partners, on the other hand, receive only 80% of the profit.

For the Limited Partners' portion of any profit-related carried interest, a hurdle rate of typically 7 to 10 percent must be overcome before the General Partner can take some or all of it. So this is how it works: You have the Private Equity firm, the General Partner, who has within it the investment team that raises the fund. The Limited Partners are investors who put money into this fund; they invest 99 percent of their funds, and one percent comes from the General Partner. The fund's capital is invested in deal firms, and they provide finance to operate those businesses and then arrange Exits, aiming for high returns.

They issue new shares, which typically have a lower value than their previous ones. But that's where it gets interesting — they take 20% of those profits and give 80% to the Limited Partners. The lifespan of a hedge fund is usually ten years, with the investment cycle ranging from five to seven years and the harvesting cycle ranging from three to five. Another thing to consider is that Private Equity firms may have on-the-ground operating partners. These are frequently seasoned executives with industry experts who assist the firm and the General Partner in deal sourcing and portfolio company management. You need to be aware that these people exist. That's the architecture of the Private Equity Company, which explains how the Limited Partners and General Partners interact and coexist.

6. Private Equity Fund Partnerships: Limited Partnerships

Let's look at a Private Equity firm's legal relationship between General and Limited Partners. Limited Partners are investors in Private Equity businesses, companies, and funds. The General Partner is the entity that finances or runs the firm. Now, the General Partner has been given control of the fund and is in charge of its investments. They are also in charge of ensuring that the Limited Partners' interests are aligned and keeping track of any potential conflicts of interest. The Limited Partners have no voice in the fund's investment decisions. Because you have a lot of different Limited Partners who each want to contribute their ideas, they'd always be someone objecting to something if they had a veto.

They have to place their faith in the General Partner, who will oversee that portion of the project. The General Partner and the Limited Partners sign a Limited Partnership agreement when the fund is created. This is the most important agreement that defines their interaction.

Limited Partners are financially liable for the entire investment in the fund. If the fund delivers a negative result, the obligations and debts are the responsibility of the General Partner. There is also an LP Clawback Clause (Limited Partner Clawback Clause), which is a provision in the Limited Partnership Agreement that says if the fund does not have enough assets to cover its obligations at some point throughout its existence, the General Partner can retrieve profits previously paid out to LPs (Limited Partners) to pay these liabilities. So, as a result, they provide some downside protection. If the whole fund goes into absolute negative territory, it becomes prudent to sell; the GPs (General Partners) are on the hook. Suppose there have been any earnings in the past and late liabilities. The General Partner can take back portions of prior distributions in that case. According to the Limited Partnership Agreement, the company is limited to a ten-year term. However, it does highlight several typical phases of the fund, which are worth noting.

The First Stage is the **Formation and organization** of the fund. There's also the **Fundraising Stage**, which typically lasts two years. Then there's a **Deal Sourcing and Investing stage** generally takes three years. **Portfolio management**, which might range from two to seven years; and finally, the **Reaping or selling** phase, which might last up to seven years. You can see how these all overlap to some extent. Those are the five critical phases of the fund's existence. The whole return structure is highly inclined to Exit their investments in this cycle. Yet, unfavorable market conditions may stifle valuations and IPO conditions, such as the dot-com bubble and bust in 2008.

When it comes to portfolio management, market timing is a crucial topic. The contract specifies the fund's investment criteria, such as industry, stage, deal type, and region. A cap restricts the maximum investment per firm within the fund. Risk diversification is also enhanced by spreading the fund's assets across multiple firms. This ensures that the fund has a balanced portfolio and benefits from diversification to better withstand market volatility.

A key-person provision is included in the agreement. The General Partner's top executives, often its most influential investors, should be included in the selection. Suppose you've got some seasoned Private Equity executives who've managed to raise the fund. In that case, you want them to stay on board if there is a significant change to the group's components. Suppose some of the most vital personnel depart. In that case, this clause allows the investment plan to be stopped so that a recruiting procedure can be completed successfully. So, the fund has a General Partner, and the firm still has a senior management group with considerable expertise. The General Partner will, as a rule, establish an advisory board to advise the fund on issues such as potential conflicts of interest, fund term extensions, and any changes to the Limited Partnership agreement. This board was created to look after the interests of the Limited Partners in connection with the General Partner and funds management. That is how the partnership agreement generally manages and regulates the relationship between Limited Partners and overall partners. You might develop a basic knowledge of this connection's functioning by going through these items. And if you're working for a Private Equity firm or will be, you'll know more about how the company keeps its investors happy.

7. Roles in a Private Equity Fund

Let's start with Executive roles in a Private Equity firm. This will give you a better understanding of the hierarchy and responsibilities at various levels within a Private Equity firm. A clear hierarchy governs the activities of Private Equity firms, which is based on roles, duties, and expertise. But unlike investment banks, Private Equity firms tend to have much flatter hierarchies because they're much smaller organizations. Young associates typically have significantly more opportunities to collaborate with more senior people, allowing them to learn faster and accept greater responsibility earlier.

Senior management roles in the company include deal origination, negotiations and closings, portfolio administration, and investment decision-making. There's also a senior position for the fundraiser, and there will always be a senior compliance officer. Junior executives will be in charge of the analytical work, producing presentations, and dealing with the specifics of transactions and transaction activity.

Now, if we begin with associates, they'll usually have a pre-MBA and will be assigned tasks like financial modeling, preliminary investigations, and providing transactional support. It's all the hard work, I'm afraid. When working in the Investment banking sector, it's easy to imagine doing many of these late nights. Even if you had to stay till two o'clock in the morning to finish it, when you were a junior, you just had to endure all of the hard work and have your director review first thing in the morning. They'll be able to tap into their existing experience and contacts in the corporate world. These candidates will help with current portfolio company work, especially if they have two to three years of investment banking or management consulting expertise already under their belts. This also aids in forming their external network before joining a company.

The Vice Presidents and Principals are effectively the marzipan layer in a business. They are in charge of deal teams. They will communicate with senior executives concerning strategy and negotiation, but they will be expected to generate good starting points. Finally, as an assistant director, I once worked with a very seasoned director who played a game called Deal of the Day. Every day, I'd have to go up to him with something completely off the wall for us to make a deal. And we'd always spend five or ten minutes discussing it, and he'd point out the flaws or advantages of it. From there, we gathered one or two leads. So it's worth doing. It also motivated me to consider the deal origin, a crucial element of any investment bank or Private Equity firm position. Vice Presidents, Senior Vice Presidents, and Principals may also share the General Partnership's carried interest. Moreover, they will be in charge of conducting due diligence procedures, directly participating in deal negotiations, and typically having an MBA from a top-tier institution.

They'll also be responsible for maintaining their external relationships with investment banks, consultants, and accounting firms. At the top, you'll find the Managing Directors and Partners, who are Senior Decision-makers and have direct involvement in portfolio firms, target companies, and investment banks. They are in charge of the company's strategy. They'll be directly involved with raising money and are expected to generate, negotiate, and finalize their investment agreements. This duty involves a significant amount of responsibility towards carried interest.

8. Understanding Management Buyout and its Intricacies

What is a Management Buyout, exactly? This is a transaction in which an owner-managed firm is purchased by a management team that has received external financing, usually from a Private Equity firm searching for current managerial buyout opportunities. In corporate restructuring, the most typical causes for an MBO are as follows:

- When a non-core business is spun out, the Management can bring in third-party investors to purchase it from the leading company where you have a founder or a controlling owner who wants to sell out or retire.
- They want to sell the firm to those who have worked alongside them, namely the management team, and allow them to do a buyout. It's either a buyout or a business sale in which the receiver administrator takes control of a viable company that is still profitable and sells it out, thus creating value for creditors of the collapsed company.

The relationships between people involved in a Management Buyout might become rather complicated since you have the seller, its counselors, and their own self-interests. You've got a purpose company, which is the entity that's established for this specific purpose. It's generally a shell firm set up to execute the purchase for the Private Equity firm or third-party financers, such as banks. There might be several of them, which makes it even more difficult. And, of course, the buyout crew is made up of various members of the team. So you have many individuals gathered around the table. Then, add that each individual and organization has its own goals. They all have different priorities. They have personal, parochial interests and expectations for what they'll receive from the transaction.

You could go even further. You have financial consultants on both sides of the table, which makes things more complicated. The due diligence advisors will advise the buyers to ensure that the company they're purchasing is of excellent quality and accuracy. Tax consultants will be a vital component of any of these transactions, and they'll play a role in the process. And, naturally, there will be much legal paperwork. So you'll need even more lawyers to put all of that together. The cash comes in the form of debt-equity. Then, you'll need loans and overdrafts to cover working capital expenditures. So, that's a lot more levels of complexity to construct.

The lending bank usually provides debt financing. This might be as high as 50% of the value of the transaction. The percentage of debt financing can range from 10 to 80 percent, and it's not uncommon for it to be as high as 70 or 80 percent. There is no one-size-fits-all approach to determining the Deal's financial structure. However, it varies from Deal to deal and is unique to each contract. Banks typically aim for the highest level of security feasible. Usually, the interest and principal repayments made by a firm's assets provide for the repayment of all debts.

The equity is divided into two parts, with the lowest risk. First, the Private Equity company puts up 40 to 50 percent of the money for the Deal. That's their cash. And it is put into the firm's equity. They can structure this money differently, but I won't delve into it. However, they may organize it in such a way that gives them a better debt position in the case that the transaction does not go through. So they have ways of protecting themselves.

They're raising the equity, putting it up beside Management in a shareholders' agreement, giving them control of that relationship. This gives them power and veto rights over the company. Even though they're working with the management team who has responsibility for the day-to-day running of the business, they have effective control.

Then, you have the Management Equity, often the smallest amount. However, the percentage maybe 5 or 10 percent of the entire sum, and it's structured to allow them to make the maximum personal capital gain from the transaction. And, of course, the equity investors are looking for Management to make cash investments. They want skin in the game, but they're more than happy to be highly incentivized to achieve a high return since that motivates them to work even harder to ensure the deals are as successful as possible. As a result, a Management Buyout (MBA) allows the Management to make a significant profit from a modest investment. And it's for this reason that they're so popular.

To summarize, a Management Buyout occurs when a company's Management purchases it, banks and the Private Equity firm finance the purchase, and Management puts in only a small amount to gain a hefty profit. That is the essence of what a Management Buyout entails.

9. What is a Leveraged Buyout, and what does it involve?

Let's look now and figure out what a Leveraged Buyout is. The good news is that the essential elements of a Leveraged Buyout are similar to those of a Management Buyout if you've decided on one. You have all of the same sorts of players. You've got the same principles. You're employing many of the same financial concepts as a Management Buyout. The distinction is that instead of a management team-led buyout of the company, a Leveraged Buyout (LBO) is a Private Equity investment fund-led buyout of a Company.

The PE firm has its financial objectives in mind and uses "**Debt**" to generate the financial returns. As a result, they refer to it as a Leveraged Buyout. A Management Buyout, on the other hand, will still result in you obtaining a Private Equity fund. You'll still be able to use Debt as needed to enhance the returns. It's all relatively straightforward, and much of it is comparable. But it'd be worth looking at a Leveraged Buyout in-depth to show how the leveraged component works.

You're a Private Equity investor who buys a company. It's a firm with Ten Million EBITDA and a five times (5X) Earnings price tag. So you spend $50 million on it, which is financed by $20 million in equity and $30 million in Debt, for a leverage ratio of 60 percent, which isn't insane. So three to five years later, the firm has 15 Million Dollars of EBITDA, and you've improved its operations. You get eight times (8X) the EBITDA when you sell it because of your efforts. So you sell it for $120 million.

Because you've had some cash flow from the company and will be able to pay down debts, if EBITDA hits 10 million dollars, you should be able to clear all of your Debt. So I've been very cautious. As a result, your Debt has been reduced to $10 million. You've got to pay off the Debt and create working capital needs and investment in the firm; nevertheless, you've made some capital repayments. The equity thus has a value of 110 million dollars. So, let's go back and pretend that you didn't utilize leverage to acquire this firm for $50 Million. You've sold it for $110 Million. You'd have made 2.2 times your investment. That's an excellent return. Not terrible. Cash on cash is a nice thing to have. Cash on cash after tax is perfect because it provides a relatively low-risk way to generate money quickly.

However, with leverage, you can earn equity out of capital that you only spent 20 million dollars on Debt and still make a 110 percent return on investment. So, your return on investment is 5.5 times greater. That's the difference, in a nutshell. The difference between the 2.2X and the 5.5X is due to the Debt you put into the company. And that is precisely what a Leveraged Buyout entails, in a nutshell. It's utilizing Debt to amplify the power of your money, which is defined as your equity. When you sell, you'll have used the cash from the firm to pay down the Debt, significantly increasing the value of your original equity investment.

10. Dispelling the Management Buyout (MBO) Myths

In this chapter, let's address some misconceptions associated with MBOs. These are infrequent occasions for businesses; most management teams will never experience them.

1. You must be a Millionaire to Acquire a Firm. This is, of course, not the case. As you learn more about how these transactions are put together, you'll discover that Venture Capitalists, Private Equity firms, and banks will be able to supply most of the money. The corporate advisors, usually Investment banks, will arrange this structure. Now, sure, the Management is expected to have a stake in the company's success after investing; however, it seldom reaches beyond five or ten percent of the purchase price and frequently not even that.

The Private Equity firm wants to know you're committed to the agreement. Still, they don't want you to be up all night worrying about whether or not you'll lose your house over it because then you won't be able to do your job effectively. The notion that MBOs can't compete with trade buyers is inconsistent with reality. It's likely that if the firm's owner is willing to sell, they'd want to sell it to someone who knew what they were doing rather than some unknown buyer from another country, corporation, or asset. Managers of adult entertainment businesses are ideally positioned to achieve this, as they should have a greater understanding of the company and the industry due to their detailed knowledge of it. They'll know immediately where all the difficulties and issues are, and they should be able to act much faster and more efficiently to complete the transaction since they won't have to do additional research. There are, of course, advantages for the workforce due to a buyout since the financial benefits may also flow down into employee share ownership.

A trade buyer may not be able to outbid a Management Buyout team. The Deal has less risk for the Management Team since they know the company so well that they should be able to pay more for it. Only exceptional Management Teams are supported by Investors. Well, the track record of Private Equity doesn't bear this out either. Many deals fail, and if they were only backing the finest teams, you'd expect them to succeed all the time. But that isn't what matters. The issue is that Private Equity firms, Venture Capital companies, and Financial Investors back balanced teams. They prefer groups with a wide range of expertise and a solid track record. Yes, leadership is essential, but they are supporting a management team. They're not investing in some wunderkind Entrepreneur.

Furthermore, suppose they entered into a transaction with someone like that running the show. In that case, they likely claim it was a high-risk business than going into an organization where there's a well-established and balanced management team and restricted sectors are bankable. So this notion that you can only conduct an MBO in a small number of sectors isn't supported by evidence; there are many different investors with various strategic goals. Almost every industry has seen MBOs, and they've seen success too. So, while one may appear accurate at first glance, it doesn't stand up under further examination.

2. Only Large Acquisitions and Huge Organizations are involved in Management Buyouts. As you will see, this is not the case. In the United Kingdom, the average buyout amount is approximately 25 million pounds. These are medium-sized businesses in general. These are branches of larger enterprises. These are affiliated companies. These are the firms that may be considered well-established. Yes, they have excellent consumers. Yes,

they have long-term revenues and cash flows, but there's room for them to develop further. It's undeniably true that some Leveraged Buyout transactions are considerably larger than others, but this is not a distinct distinction. There are several medium-sized Leveraged Buyouts as well.

3. MBOs are Risky. However, they are not always more dangerous than other transactions. It is entirely based on how they're structured. Make sure you don't overpay, that you don't have leverage, and have reasonable cash flows, which we can pay down and deal with your debt service. It also helps to have a well-thought-out, well-planned growth strategy. So you can't justly state that MBOs are more dangerous but not risk-free.

You have a few of the MBO misconceptions I hope we've laid to rest there. I hope it aids you in gaining a more balanced perspective on the potential of an MBO.

11. Glossary of Investors

To begin our journey through a glossary of investors, there is much jargon in the world of Private Equity; as I've already said, I'd like to take you on a stroll through some distinct sorts of investors so you can see how they connect in the mosaic. We begin with an **Incubator**, which is a business that gives startup businesses space and resources to assist them in getting up and running. In comparison, they cannot provide a substantial amount of money. It might be anywhere from $20,000 to $30,000. Still, they offer mentorship, networking introductions, and assistance locating essential partners and investors. Y Combinator is an excellent example. If a company has completed its training program, it is much more likely to find investors for its next growth stage.

You may have heard the term "**Bootstrapping**." You're funding your business from your resources, such as your credit cards. You're pulling yourself up by your bootstraps if you don't have access to external funding. High-net-worth individuals are Angel Investors, typically and frequently successful entrepreneurs. They aren't professional Venture Capitalists or Private Equity investors. They are not wealthy individuals who seek to buy their way into the company through financial investment. They mostly use their own money to finance their investments. The typical investment is around 250,000 Dollars, whereas the usual investment is 500,000 Dollars. They frequently seek a fantastic piece of the pie, perhaps around a third of the equity in a young firm. So you enlist their help because they provide vital liquidity during the company's development. However, they do have a hefty price tag. They frequently wish to be on the board and closely watch what's going on in the organization to ensure that their funds are being spent effectively.

The first tranche of professional investors, then, is **Venture Capital**. VC funds generally invest a minor portion of their money in fast-growing early-stage firms. They're frequently businesses that have already generated revenue but are still in the early stages of becoming profitable. So they have negative cash flow, so they seek venture capital financing. They can't borrow money because they don't have any profits or a positive cash flow. As a result, the job of the venture capital firm is to assist. These are high-risk, high-reward transactions.

The next stage is **Growth Equity**, which is similar to Venture Capital. We've seen Private Equity firms invest in the minority or sometimes majority stakes in early-stage enterprises, with the goal of transforming less developed businesses into market leaders based on their innovative business models or technology. They're trying to acquire a company that has a product that has been proven in the market. So they've got consumers. They discovered that it works, sells well, and wants to expand the firm dramatically. And that's what they're looking for.

I want to draw your attention to the funding for **Mezzanine finance** since it's closely related. However, you must first understand where it sits in the pecking order. Specialist Private Equity firms fund it. It's typically restricted to junior or subordinated Debt. It's under the senior Debt and above the Private Equity funds; therefore, it's in the middle of both categories. In terms of seniority and ranking, they are usually worth 15% or 20%. They are frequently accompanied or may be provided with warrants to convert into equity or options. So, they have an extra equity stake. Typically, mezzanine financing is employed to bridge the gap when senior Debt is not accessible to the extent that the lead investor Private Equity firm desires. So you're talking about mezzanine finance investors, who fill in a gap in the funding structure rather than the funding timetable.

This concludes our discussion of Venture Capital, and we now come to Private Equity firms, so there's a lot to say about this. In future chapters, I'll go through a variety of buyouts. But they are critical, representing a collection of businesses that specialize in many investment techniques. We'll discuss those geographies and industries and how much money you may invest, ranging from Millions to Billions. They're the heart of the Buyout market, as you can see. However, this concept has several different types and modifications, which is why I'll look at buyout transactions in a separate section.

We now arrive at the **Family offices**. These are "Investment firms" in inverted commas, which are established by a wealthy family and professionally manage their investments. They're a form of Private Equity, to put it another way. They are more long-term in nature. Also, because they're often not looking to make realizations, but to build up asset portfolios of firms that they typically hold for a long time, these types of investors frequently aren't seeking opportunities.

Strategic Investors are already existing firms, so we're referring to other businesses investing in early-stage startups to access new technology or business models. Now, they frequently take the place of a Venture Capitalist. They will arrive with a joint venture structure or, in the end, come in with an option and the intention to buy the firm entirely because they want the technology or wish to expand it. They allow potential investors to grow a firm during its early phases, allowing its founders to profit before they bring it in-house.

Another category of investors is **Corporate Venture Capital**, which invests in large corporations and does so opportunistically or as part of a formal program. They target early-stage company firms, frequently with cutting-edge technology. So they've established an Intel-like structure, and it's put up a department with perhaps a Billion Dollars in investment. And, to allow it access to cutting-edge technology later on, it wanted to concentrate on early-stage IT firms. It's a method of assisting firms in developing. It's also a way to prevent other businesses from stealing innovative technology while asleep. These are significant investors that are looking for the long term. They're seeking long-term success with this technology and providing financing to assist these new firms in crowd-funding creation.

It's worth noting because, in recent years especially, it has become a highly successful method for young startup companies to raise non-institutional cash on relatively informal terms. It's a fundraising campaign for small amounts of money from a large number of generally nameless investors to finance the development of a startup prototype or some other sort of new business, such as Kickstarter and Indiegogo. However, you're a young Startup business. In that case, consider before giving a third of your firm to an Angel Investor or a Venture Capital fund.

These are the leading players in the private company investment market, and as you can see, they're already well beyond traditional Venture Capital and Private Equity firms. Even more so, those two categories have grown more complicated in nature. They have become more specialized in their approach and more strategically motivated than they were 20 years ago. That is precisely what makes the market so intriguing. So, after reading this little detour into the many sorts of investors you'll encounter in this market, you'll better understand how they all connect.

12. Glossary of Buyout Terms

We've already learned that Private Equity investors are complicated. Their methods and techniques can be complex, so it's worth looking at various phrases that describe buyouts to understand better what they're talking about. I want to take your knowledge of the world of buyouts a step further. I want to do so in more depth because there are several different sorts of deal agreements with which the word Leveraged Buyout or LBO is used. However, if you look deeper into them, you will find that they have certain qualities in common. The more intriguing nuances and complexities of the world of acquisitions begin to emerge.

Let's begin with the most basic **Leveraged Buyout (LBO)** form and work our way up. A Leveraged Buyout, or LBO, is a transaction that uses Debt as collateral to raise money. It's generally for bigger, more mature enterprises. It incorporates the acquisition of a firm by a Private Equity or Buyout Company. This is the same as saying that you have a legal responsibility to pay for any repairs or maintenance that might be required, but only if it's due to an accident caused by someone else. You'll also hear the phrase concerning this business automobile, defined as the other side of the bargain. A Public corporation occasionally sells a non-core division. To a Strategic buyer, it severs part of itself or non-core assets. It may be another company in a different sector or a financial buyer like EPF.

This is where the roles of Corporate Buyers and Sellers and Private Equity firms come together. When a firm carve-out is involved, it's assumed to be the work of a Private Equity company. Another option is an MBO, a **Management Buyout**, which is still a Leveraged Buyout in which the current Management purchases the company from its parent with the aid of a Private Equity firm. This is critical because the Management understands the company well and works with a Private Equity firm's partnership to execute a Leveraged Buyout. The Management, after all, has a piece of the action, and they're hoping to profit alongside the Private Equity firm while leveraging the arrangement.

Management Buy-in (MBI) is a Management Buyout when a person or entire management team from the outside comes in and purchases a current firm. This is a high-risk offer because the new management teams don't have the same business knowledge as the old ones. As a result, if there are any skeletons in the closet after the transaction closes, they'll only discover them then.

A BIMBO is a cross between an MBO and an MBI. It's when a senior executive joins forces with the existing Management of a firm to finalize the acquisition. The senior guy comes in from the outside and collaborates with the current Management. A Private Equity firm subsequently finances the transaction after it has been accomplished. Middle-market buyouts are a catchall phrase for the range of players that operate in this market. Essentially, they take over mid-market firms to acquire them. Typically, the target companies have revenues of 25 million to One Billion dollars. But you'll hear it bandied about. It's any trade of that magnitude or larger. And it has nothing to do with the strategies we've discussed. You'll like this one much more. And I wanted to include it for a change of pace.

Limited Partners have used the term "JAMBOG" to refer to a middle-market buyout firm that has failed to distinguish itself. JAMBOG is the name of a firm that specializes in middle-market buyouts. But it would be a good idea to include something lighthearted like this.

Let's look at **Secondary Buyouts** now because what we've discussed till now are mostly Primary purchases. A Secondary buyout is the purchase of a company by another Private Equity firm that a Private Equity firm has previously funded. So it's a secondary transaction, the primary transactions being the first PE investment and another PE firm buying the company from the original PE investor. There are also specialist businesses that specialize in secondary sales. An already Private Equity financed firm is sold to another company rather than a strategic or trade buyer. This allows the original PE business to obtain immediate liquidity without going through an IPO or a complicated trade sale.

We'll start with a **Direct Secondary** and get quite technical. Still, you'll hear these words, and knowing what they imply is beneficial. A Secondary transaction is one in which the stockholder in a privately owned firm that a PE firm has previously backed sells their portion to another individual Limited Partner or PE firm. So, for example, a particular stockholder sells only their stake in a privately funded company backed by a Private Equity firm. It's a Direct Second. You're investing in the company being sold by a stockholder directly.

This is just the beginning. The fund has two other types of Limited Partners: LPs and Investors. A Limited Partner sells its proportionate interest in the fund as a whole or a firm to a third party via an **LP Secondary** or an **Investor Secondary**, respectively. So, in the LP, they are differentiated by the fact that, secondarily, the fund. Second, it's the limited partner who's selling.

A **Synthetic Secondary** occurs when a limited partner sells its economic interests and liabilities but not the legal ownership of the fund structure. So it stays in the fund structure, but it's transferred to a third party, which is why banks are interested. It just remains in the middle since that's where we began. It makes the arrangement more straightforward. However, there are always possibilities for Deal structuring to be innovative, as I'm sure you can comprehend. Secondary transactions are also conceivable. At this point, a third-party Limited Partner enters the picture by wanting to invest in a specific Private Equity fund. They can also occur for capital cash flow or portfolio balance reasons. So, I hope you found this little digression on buyout conditions beneficial. You begin to grasp some of the intricacies in Primary Buyouts and the Complex market that spins around in Secondary Buyout markets.

13. Glossary of Investment Terms

Let's go through some investment phrases related to Private Equity and buyouts, which are typically used in particular situations. This is a small collection of investment phrases that pertain to buyout transactions. However, as you can see, we're adding more detail and complexity to the whole world of buyouts.

1. These four terms all mean the same thing: **Development, Capital growth, Capital expansion, and Equity.** The basic idea is that a Private Equity firm might invest in an organization to assist it in scale, which amounts to many things. These are all phrases that refer to the same scenario: a PE firm investing in a firm to help it scale.
2. Series: It's the first institutional round of investment, commonly known as a series.
3. A Take-Private transaction is a method by which a Private Equity firm acquires a public company, then delists the company and reverts to being privately held. The other name for this is a public-private transaction. This is where Bridge finance or a bridge loan comes into play. Its money is made available to a company by investors until such time as the firm raises its next investment round. Bridge financing comes into play in scenarios where it takes longer than expected to close the round or if there's a sudden need for short-term funding for a specific project or product. It's usually organized as convertible Debt, which converts into equity in the following investment round, and it does so on favorable terms.
4. A Club deal is a financing arrangement in which two Private Equity firms join forces to invest in the firm. This could be due to a lack of capital from one or both Private Equity firms, because the deals are too large to invest in alone, or because the two have complementary skill sets. It's a company turnaround, or you need to know more about a specific market or sector. In any case, organizations are frequently acquainted with each other. Former employees of competing firms may also bring them together. This is where two PE firms combine forces to complete the transaction. A limited partner (LP) invests directly in the portfolio company, alongside the PE firm, rather than through the fund. So, it's a limited partner investment into the company.
5. A Pipe is a public investment in Private Equity. This was primarily confined to the United States market before. It's often an unquoted instrument developed by the public business for the Private Equity firm, and it's usually a reasonably small amount of money. The instrument does not carry an imputed price, but it is designed to produce the same level of investment return as Private Equity. It allows a public company to access cash without going back on the market frequently for a specific strategy or cause. It's all about market timing. And the stock markets aren't open to more equity. Whatever it is, it allows the public corporation to access Private Equity money uniquely.
6. Roll-Up or Buy then Build: Now, this is a term that is sometimes used interchangeably when a Private Equity firm takes on the strategy of acquiring a platform business and then making a series of acquisitions against the competition in order to either gain market leadership or at the very least significantly boost returns through scale. A Private Equity organization is acquiring and building up competitors to create a larger business.
7. Add-ons or extras are one of the many items you acquire when you buy an app. It's comparable to a build-bought-in, but it might be just once rather than part of a plan.

Now, for completeness, alternative assets outside the realm of bank bonds or publicly traded equities include hedge funds, commodities, and derivatives. But, of course, it also covers Private Equity and Venture Capital. It covers buyouts, mezzanines, and other issues we've discussed. These are all alternative assets.

8. **Money in and out** refers to the flow of cash: When a PE firm purchases stock directly from a business owner who takes the cash out of the firm and deposits it in his account. So he's not putting the money back into the firm. He's taking money off the table, a synonym for cash out or money out.
9. When an investor who has made a preliminary investment in a firm invests in the next financing round, it's called a **Follow-on investment**. To prevent dilution in the transaction, they make this kind of investment frequently. This is most often a write included in the original loan's conditions. It is an alternative. It's not a legal requirement, but they can continue to ensure that the initial investment isn't value jeopardized or diluted by subsequent financing rounds.
10. A turnaround is an investment in a firm in financial difficulties to help it recover and become profitable. If a business is not performing well, the owner may be bankrupt or in administration. When a company is in bankruptcy, the first cost may be low (sometimes zero), and the aim is often to turn a profit when it becomes profitable again. However, the complexity of the issue can be time-consuming and costly to implement.

These are some investment terms in general, which you should be aware of. You can at least comprehend what they're talking about when you hear them.

14. What is a Fund of Funds?

In this chapter, we'll discuss the benefits and drawbacks of Limited Partners investing in Funds of funds. So, what exactly are Funds of funds? The Private Equity funds that invest in other Private Equity funds and those other Private Equity funds that make direct investments into businesses is a typical Fund of funds loop. Limited Partners benefit from a broader diversification in their investment portfolio since they have access to various Private Equity funds, each with its own set of criteria. At the time a Limited Partner invests in a fund of funds, it is frequently an unknown pool. This implies that when the Limited Partners invest in a fund of funds, they won't know which Private Equity firms the fund will invest in.

In some instances, a fund of funds may provide a target list of Venture Capital or Private Equity funds to invest in. Now, this does not guarantee that those investments will be made. Still, it does provide the Limited Partner a clearer view of the underlying Private Equity or Venture firms that may have stakes in them. Now, fund of funds and Private Equity funds operate on a committed capital basis, so it's worth briefly explaining what committed capital is and how it works.

The total amount of money available to a committee is its capital. The amount of capital the Limited Partners paid in at any one moment is called their total capital commitment. Typically, what happens with a fund is that there's a National Capital Call. Then, further Capital Calls are made over time. So the "Called Capital" is everything paid in a specific period. This means the "Un-called Capital" is the net of Committee-capital minus the Called-capital. It's the fund's remaining cash reserves, which they can draw on from their Limited Partners. The most fundamental difference is that the management fee is only linked to the amount of cash that has been committed.

What are the advantages of investing in a fund of funds for a limited partner? First, let's start with the basics. Funds of funds offer more diversification because the investments across several Private Equity funds are all linked to underlying portfolio companies. When the risk-adjusted return is calculated, it may be improved by diversifying more. Now, because the fund-to-fund investment team can analyze the target funds they want to invest in, they will have a leg up on their competition. The Limited Partners, on the other hand, may not have access to this information or expertise and must trust the fund. Many funds have special interests that allow them to profit from them without hiring outside advice while maintaining a diversified portfolio that lowers their risk.

The General Partner of the fund funds takes care of all capital calls from the invested funds. They may also execute distributions when investors get shares, stock, or other non-cash assets from their invested funds instead of receiving cash. A fund of funds is a structure in which the General Partner invests money raised by other Limited Partners and distributes it to those Limited Partners. The ultimate goal for the fund of funds structure is simplicity for investors. Because all the Limited Partners must manage only one fund, they handle any issues with calls or distributions. A small Limited Partner may gain access to a single investment to a broad range of Private Equity.

The next alternative is to invest in a Private Equity fund. However, these are often limited to a minimum investment of approximately five million dollars. For inexperienced investors, a fund of funds might be an excellent low-risk entry into the Private Equity asset class. However, there are some things to consider before investing in a fund of funds.

Funds of funds must create their own money, charge their management fee, and carry, which effectively doubles the limited partner's costs. These are the funds they're investing in and the funds from which they're getting their money. When diversified and adjusted, the risk-return profile may be lower than that of a direct investment in a PE fund. However, it can also result in reduced returns. Limited Partners will have less influence and fewer opportunities to interact with fund managers in the funds. The fund of funds will manage the relationship.

A fund of funds may experience a longer and deeper J-Curve. This term is frequently used in the early phases of the investment cycle, particularly in Venture funds. So they put money into the fund, but its net asset value often goes down before recovering and possibly even falling below its initial threshold during the investment cycle as the underlying businesses begin to perform and become more valuable. It also forms a standard J shape, with a fund of funds having a larger and more experienced J-Curve to invest directly in Private Equity.

The Limited Partners will have significantly less information about the underlying businesses in the various portfolios of the funds to which the fund funds have invested. Finally, while there is a secondary market for Limited Partners, positions in PE funds are less liquid than Fund of funds or Limited Partner investments. This implies that if a limited partner wants to sell its fund, it must take a greater discount on net asset value than if the position was held directly in a Private Equity fund.

That concludes our overview of funds of funds, a complex subject. It's worth noting that while some funds may offer investors more choice and diversity in portfolio construction than others, every fund has certain standard features like minimum investment levels or strategies used to invest the money. So that's a quick intro to funds of funds, particularly from a Limited Partner perspective. It also addresses the advantages and disadvantages of investing in funds of funds rather than directly in Private Equity as a Limited Partner.

Section 3: The Characteristics of Private Equity Firms That Must Be Recognized

15. Categorizing Private Equity Firms

Let's get into how we can categorize Private Equity firms. If you grasp the logic behind categorization, you'll better understand the structure of the Private Equity market. It's easiest to differentiate PE Firms by the type of businesses, the magnitude, and the kinds of transactions they're involved in. It may appear quite simple, but remember that it is rather complicated. But if I give you a few pointers for these criteria, you can tell if a business does or doesn't do something. That way, you'll better understand Private Equity firms' position in the Industry.

You can start by understanding that there are three primary types of Private Equity firms: Leveraged Buyout Companies and Venture Capital Companies. In between, we have Growth Equity Firms. The first thing to consider for Private Equity Leveraged Buyout firms is that they usually **acquire controlling stakes** in firms and seek larger, more established organizations with stable, preferably increasing cash flow since they require recurring income to fund their debt repayments. This loan aims to fund operations while the company grows and establishes a track record. They're usually financed with a combination of Debt and Equity, and the balance between Debt and Equity varies considerably depending on the business and market conditions. Kohlberg Kravis Roberts (KKR), Carlyle Group, TPG, and Blackstone are examples of big Leveraged Buyout firms.

The Venture Capital firms usually invest minority stakes in early-stage Startups. The Startup could be "Pre-revenue," and each round of funding could be part of a Series (Series A, B, C). *These are funding rounds that typically get the most attention in TechCrunch, Inc42, and other media outlets that cover Startup stories*. The Series classification helps to categorize, name, and number funding rounds, such as the initial. You'll also notice that the composition of investors' interests changes as these rounds progress. There will be companies that are happy to invest earlier in higher-risk, higher-return projects. There are also a few more risk-averse firms that will only invest in the C or D rounds. They'll generally invest considerably more money. However, given that they'll be more established and bigger, with better financial attributes than venture capital firms are looking for, the businesses will have received a significant boost. They're searching for intellect, innovation, and inventive technology that have the potential to provide them with a high return. So it's an entirely different business. There are many examples of VC firms: Kleiner Perkins, Sequoia Capital, Accel Partners, August Capital, and Andreessen Horowitz.

Growth Equity companies that fall in between. They are seeking more established corporations. What they're searching for, however, is to get in at the point when these firms want to expand. It's after the VC rounds. These companies are not yet mature enough for typical Private Equity firms. So, they're a link between the two. They'll bring in a combination of Debt and Equity, but the Debt will be restricted to the level the firms can afford. These deals will typically result in more Equity because they are attempting to develop the firm rather than seeking a financially engineered return, as evidenced by Summit Partners.

Let's look at another perspective for these businesses: What kind of business would they want to acquire? Large, mid-market or small businesses are the focus of our discussion; by that, I mean a company with revenues of more than $1 Billion or $150 Million or less than $150

Million. If you look at the agreements they've made and the firms that a particular Private Equity firm has acquired, you'll have some indication of which sector they're playing in.
Many companies have a sector focus, as many industries are highly complicated.
Suppose you don't have sector knowledge. You won't be able to evaluate whether the company you're buying will achieve the returns that satisfy your expectations in that market. In that case, it's as simple as this. Typical industries that PE Firms operate in are Health Care, Technology, Fast-Moving Consumer Goods (FMCG), Retail, Financial Services, and pretty much any other sector you can think of. Industry specialization is a Major Theme within the realm of Private Equity. There are a few generalists, but most firms are becoming specialists.

Let's look at some of the Deal types that they can perform. This can get quite complicated quickly, so pay attention. **Leveraged Buyout firms** typically evaluate carve-out arrangements. *These are essentially acquisitions of non-core or a subsidiary or a division of a larger business that is then invested in and developed.* They're searching for a way to put power behind these. They want them to have good cash flow characteristics so that they may benefit from the financial Leverage. The difference between **Buy and Build** firms is minor. This is when Growth Equity enters the picture, with the company acquiring a platform firm before making acquisitions of smaller firms to scale it up and expand it through a mix of Equity and Debt. A corporation will buy a public firm listed on a stock exchange to take it private to take control of its Equity. It is true that minorities are rarely included in these collaborations. They'll provide management with some equity as an incentive. However, the objective is to develop that firm privately before selling it in three to five years via Public listing.

Management Buyouts (MBOs) are also seen in acquisitions where a company's founder sells to a Private Equity firm, allowing the management to take control. However, without the investors, the management would not have the financial means to provide the founder with a quick exit. And in addition to all of this, there's also a **Management Buy-in**. An external management team enters a high-risk or difficult-to-do business. In addition, you'll notice some of the following: Specialist funds that invest in difficult situations and specialist arrangements. Specialist contracts, distressed transactions, and turnaround deals are just a few examples.

There are **real estate-focused Investment funds**. There are **Mezzanine finance-focused investment funds**. This is a debt with a very high coupon that's subordinated to the primary loan. In certain circumstances, it may be exchanged for Equity or come with a warrant or some premium to provide them with an equity carry. There are **Funds of funds**, which are Private Equity Fund businesses that invest in other PE firms so that they may invest. But they're contributing some of the ownership. **Secondary Investors** buy existing Private Equity transactions rather than starting their own. However, the lifespan of most funds that obtain funds is generally ten years. There may be just a few firms left in the fund. The Secondary fund, on the other hand, will come in and buy those firms for them. Then, as a final example, there are **pre-IPO funds** that provide the business with some cash before it goes public. They won't be able to IPO without it. The **IPO funds**, on the other hand, provide the experts with the cash they require. Turnaround Money, Recapitalizations, and different situations are also unique funds that focus on specific types of complex transactions.

This gives you an idea of the many Private Equity businesses available. It's critical to have an overall understanding of Private Equity in this regard. In the upcoming chapters, we'll dive deeper into Leveraged Buyout funds and Management Buyout firms to understand those transactions. Also, this is your first encounter with this aspect of Corporate Finance. In that case, it's okay to read what we have covered several times. It can get a bit overwhelming. Work with me and I will take you past the finish line.

16. The Differences between Private Equity & Venture Capital Deal Stages

Understanding the fundamental difference between a Venture Capital and a Private Equity firm is crucial to Corporate Finance. This difference boils down to "Two" words; "Deal-Stage." Depending on your company's stage, you'll be able to understand better what type of Funds can help you best. The graphic below summarizes it succinctly.

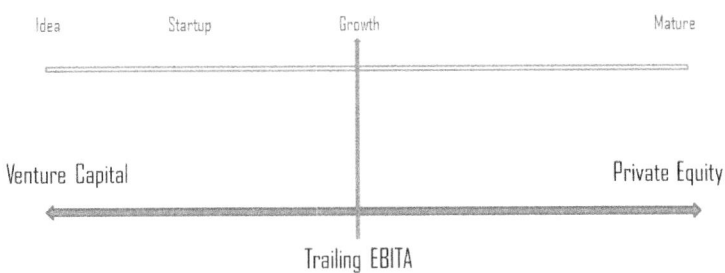

The top line traces the progress of a Company's Maturity from Idea through Startup, Growth, and Maturity. The blue line on the bottom is when a company begins to make money and generate prior earnings. EBITDA is a widely used profit measurement. EBITDA is earnings before Maintenance Expenses, Interest payments on Debt, and Depreciation. It's a short way of saying "Operational Cashflow". But I don't want to go into the nitty-gritty details. It is this EBITDA, i.e., earnings figure, that both "Venture Capital" and "Private Equity" firms are interested in. When a firm reaches a particular stage in its growth where it can look back 12 months, 18 months, or two years and show historical EBITDA performance, it has evolved into a Private Equity space firm from the Venture Capital space. There are many different types of deals they may do.

If you consider EBITDA (earnings before interest, tax, depreciation, and amortization), ask yourself whether this firm has a track record of past trailing EBITDA profits. If the answer is "Yes", then it's a good fit for Private Equity. If the answer is "No," you must look for Venture Capital. The distinction between PE and VC is that the latter invests in early-stage companies.

17. A Private Equity Firm's Life Cycle

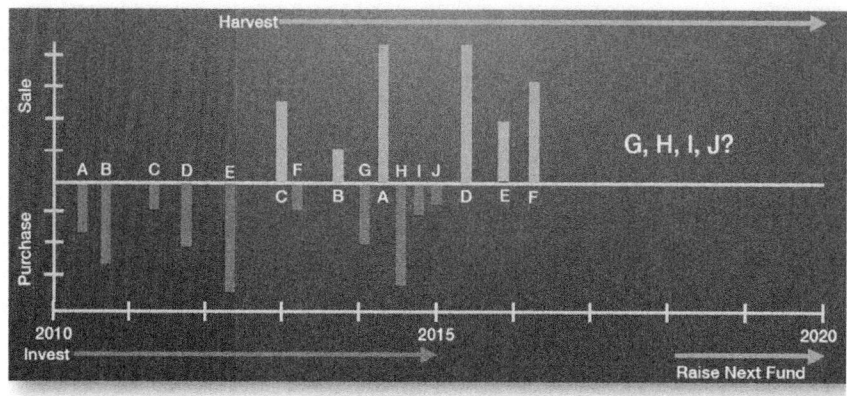

We've already discussed that Private Equity firms seek money for Buyouts, which is a straightforward statement. Each fund is itself an SPV (Special Purpose Vehicle). It's a business dedicated to certain investors, with stringent conditions and the goal of being the company's investment vehicle and that of its financial partners. In other words, the returns on these investments are typically restricted to ten years in order for the fund to repay or reimburse all of its investors their earnings and, hopefully, make a profit for them at the end of ten years. Of course, they may lose money.

The process follows: The Private Equity fund issues prospectuses, sells stock to investors, raises a Special Purpose Vehicle with 100 Million Dollars, for example, and establishes an SPV. It then goes into a phase of investing the cash, developing the businesses, selling the firms, and taking in the profit. The Profits are returned to shareholders after taking their returns and commissions throughout the next ten years. This strategy will generally start around year eight, as it takes approximately 18 months to raise the next fund and draw in new investors based on its track record and first fund's success.

This is an example of how the process works, and there are two phases: Investment and Harvest. In this scenario, the Red cash flow indicates they're putting money into their investment accounts. You can also see that they've made ten investments since today. The Green is when they sell the securities and earn a positive cash return, usually in the majority of situations. In the case of their first sale, businesses learn that they bought it for a modest sum of money and made three times what they paid. But, with Company B, they've done the polar opposite. They've acquired it for a significant sum but haven't seen much of a return on their investment. That's typical of an investment profile. Not every deal will succeed, and they're aiming for a long-term return of around 20% to 30% for their investors over the whole portfolio. So that's what the cash flows look like. And that's how you may think of a fund.

Private Equity Firm Lifecycle

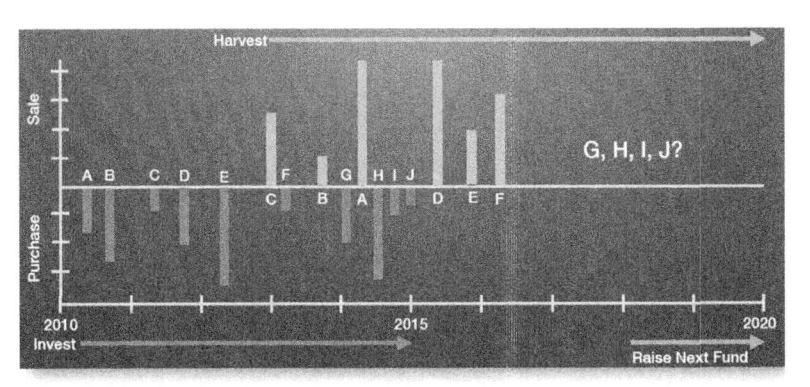

We've still got firms G, H, I, and J to sell. As they approach their 10-year mark, these firms will begin shopping for a secondary vehicle to assist them in selling their businesses and closing the fund down so that investors can get their cash back. That's a glimpse into the life cycle of a fund. It will provide insight into how Private Equity investors think of their investments as a portfolio and how the passage of time, duration, and life cycle affect their behavior.

18. How Do Private Equity Firms Create Value?

How Do Private Equity Firms Create Value? If you understand this, you'll have a leg up on how they structure their agreements. There are three primary methods by which Private Equity firms generate value. They combine any of the three approaches to get the overall return and result.

The three strategies are:

1. Operational Improvement
2. Multiple Arbitrage
   &
3. Leverage

The Operational turnaround speaks for itself. They improve an organization's operations in order to make it more efficient. That is likely to happen if they expand the product line. They offer loans to new markets. They may make acquisitions and savings in any way possible. They may restructure the management team, reorganize the organizational structure, seek better terms of existing Debt from banks, seek supplier-level incentives, and improve account receivables. They'll raise prices, cut costs, and do whatever it takes to improve their bottom line.

At the core of all Arbitrage Opportunities is Financial Engineering. Multiple Arbitrage is a form of financial engineering. This also implies that, when they buy the company, they acquire it on a multiple of four or five times EBITDA. However, when they sell the company, they ensure it is sold for at least six, seven, or eight times EBITDA. The consequence is that for every Dollar of revenue a firm earns on day one, it gains more value, regardless of the business's success. As long as the firm makes a Dollar of profit, it will receive more value back for that Dollar of profit than it paid for it. So if a firm has $100 of profit and purchases it for four times that amount, they spend $400. In five years, profit has only remained at $100. They sell eight times (8X) for $800 each. And in the meantime, the business has done nothing. They've increased their company's return by two times (2X). They've purchased for four hundred and sold for eight hundred.

Leverage is when a company uses Debt to partially finance the transaction, implying that they use their revenue stream to pay down the Debt during their ownership. This means that if they buy a business on 50/50 Debt-Equity and in the period of ownership, they repay all of the Debt and double the equity value. That's where "Operational Improvement," "Multiple Arbitrages," and "Leverage" come in. Now, owing to changing market conditions and the savvy of managers, the influence and interaction of these three elements have evolved.

In the 1980s, Leverage was all the rage. In the 1990s, it was more about multiple arbitrages. It's been more about increasing earnings in the 2000s, however, without being particularly sophisticated. In the last eight years, there's been a lot more hands-on work to do with the company's specific development in order to boost value through greater profitability and earnings.

Let's have a look at each of these in more depth. Most value was generated by Private Equity firms in the 1990s using Leverage. An excellent example of this is KKR Kohlberg Kravis Roberts, who acquired RJR Nabisco largely debt-leveraged, primarily through the use of junk bonds and junk bonds were the talk of the town that month. They were highly subordinated instruments with high yields but allowed buyout firms to fund otherwise hard-to-find transactions. Junk bonds were discredited during the 1990s, and the game was to buy low and sell high. It was about the company's value and a multiplicity of Arbitrage. In the 2000s, there was a lot more attention on growing earnings. Still, it was mainly through basic activities like cost-cutting, acquisition, and divestiture to reduce firm Leverage. It was not, however, anything particularly sophisticated, and it's only recently that buyout firms have had to work much harder. And this is mainly because big banks, particularly since 2008, have been able to offer relatively little Leverage.

Sellers and purchasers are savvier today than they were in the past about selling to Private Equity and purchasing from Private Equity. As a result, they must roll up their sleeves and work harder to improve the company and operations to make it more valuable. So that is a summary. This is very significant to Private Equity value creation. I hope you find this information valuable and engaging and that it goes some way toward explaining or understanding how Private Equity firms typically structure their transactions and why they do so.

19. The Measurement of Private Equity and Compensation

Let's examine how Private Equity firms measure their Performance and Pay metrics.

- What major ways a company might use data to improve its operations?
- How do they expect their investors to perform?
- What are their requirements for returns for their investors?
- What are their overall financial goals, and how do they achieve them?

Don't forget that they're running a portfolio, and in general, they're seeking a variety of returns across the portfolio. They know that not every transaction will be a home run. Let's assume that they land ten deals in their fund during the course of a portfolio. They'd want two blockbusters, great deals, with low investment and a high return. At a minimum, you'll make money back three (3X), four (4X), or five times (5X) what you invested. Making a 4X ROI (Return on Investment) is an excellent result per the Private Equity benchmark. Venture Capital investors anticipate earning even better returns. They look for ten times (10X) returns on occasion. They're putting money into the company earlier than Private Equity investors. They're putting their money to work at a greater level of intensity. They anticipate bigger profits.

Let's dial back on Private Equity at the moment. So they're after one deal that will triple their money, which means they'll look at ten blockbusters and only want one superstar, a couple of deals that will double their money, and three deals that will provide them with a single figure, single cash. They get their money back, a single return deal on their investment. The final two deals, on the other hand, are failures. The bank took the keys away. They anticipate that they will lose their cash, that is, the type of spread they search for.

The Internal Rate of Return (IRR) is how investors assess their returns. The cash return is another method for measuring returns. The internal rate of return is the amount of money that needs to double in value over a specific time to equal the return.

Consider another way of phrasing it. You take your beginning and ending points, divide them, and then discount them to arrive at the starting point. You need to reduce by 30% to reach the number from the end to the start. So it's a statement of how much money has grown over time. It's a mathematical calculation. The problem is that IRRs are very sensitive to the period and change rapidly. You can set up an IRR if you have a contract, invest $10M, and get out $100M over ten years. You'll be going through it ten times in ten years, which isn't even comparable to double your money every year. But you're growing up in a steady, consistent manner. If you do it in ten minutes, the IRR will be enormous. It's susceptible to the return's time frame.

Private Equity firms are increasingly talking about their cash returns, which they define as "the rate of return on an asset over a given period of time." If they reach an agreement for 100, they will put in 30 of their Equity and borrow the rest. In the period after the investment, they'll attempt to get equity value back, maybe 60 or 90 or more. And it's done by operational improvements aided by financial Leverage. It is produced by growth development, by Arbitrage on their entry and exit values. A cash return is a more accurate way to assess outcomes for Private Equity investments.

The next topic on hand is:

- How do Private Equity firms make money?

- What does their compensation structure look like?

It's divided into two parts. The first component is a **Management fee**, usually 2% of the fund's yearly returns. **Deal fees** are charged when they negotiate one. **Directors' fees** are paid to them. However, due to the amount of money that they hope to generate in the future, it is insignificant when compared to their ultimate objectives. It covers the essentials and, more importantly, pays the salaries and rent and keeps the lights on. The remaining return component is their **Carried Interest**, which is generally between 15 and 20% of profits on the distribution of returns above a hurdle rate. This means that when the fund is closed, investors want to get their initial investment back first and then receive a built-in rate of return. They also want to make a profit on top of that. Then 20% or 15% of the remaining funds go to the Private Equity firm in terms of carried interest, and the rest is shared among investors in the fund.

If they do really well, they may make a lot of money since the bulk of the profits go to the top. There are known to be a few Managing Directors and Directors in Private Equity firms. This concludes the discussion of Private Equity measurement and compensation. It lets you see what type of profits Private Equity is striving for. And it also reveals how Private Equity firms make money. Another thing to note is that you can use this analysis to figure out how they'll evaluate offers and what they'll get rewarded for the time and effort they put into them.

Section 4: The Right Private Equity Firm to Work With

20. How to Find Investor-Deal Fit

How to find the right investor for your firm? There are numerous stages to the fundraising process, and due diligence is given for each. It's best to contact several firms before deciding so you can compare their offers and determine which one will provide you with the greatest return on investment. The criteria that Venture Capital and Private Equity companies use in order to evaluate potential investments vary. Still, they are continuously published on their websites. If you're considering approaching a financial investor, read it thoroughly. So that's where you'll start. But allow me to go a bit deeper with you.

The primary financial investment criteria are usually assessed on three main factors. **Industry Sector** Businesses and Investor Enterprises have recognized that investing knowledge in specific fields is primarily profitable. *Pre-IPO Investors can be exempted from this rule. They tend to be businesses with diverse methods for solving problems in a less-defined sector, such as pre-IPO investors.* But, for all purposes and intents, be sure that your sector and subsector(s) are consistent with the investment criteria of the investor you wish to approach.

Second, it is incredibly **Stage-Dependent**; therefore, certain VCs will only invest in early-stage investments or series that are cash flow positive. Private Equity firms are no different. Secondary buyouts are not uncommon. Some firms will only work on secondary development transactions. For example, Management Buy-in (MBI) is how some businesses would describe it.

So, once again, you must ensure that your firms are at the correct development level for the firm you wish to contact.

Finally, **Geography** is Key. Look for a firm's local office and a map of the region. So long as you're in London, that's fine if there's a major Californian business with an office in London if they don't have a London office and just one in San Francisco, which isn't going to work. It's widely accepted that the closer the investment connection in geographic terms, the smaller the deal, and vice versa. This is particularly true since the amounts of money are smaller. As a result, if there is a lot of commuting between the two locations, it becomes increasingly difficult for both persons to keep up with each other and maintain the connection. As a result, geographic proximity is a crucial factor to consider.

Bear in mind that **demand from entrepreneurs outstrips supply from investors**; to put it another way, Venture Capitalists and Private Equity firms have more chances than they can handle. They'll examine 500 transactions during the year, of which they'll look at 100 in detail and have meetings. They'll spend their time studying a typical firm and looking at as many as 500 deals, with the goal of finding one or two that are major enough to schedule a meeting about. Typically, they will invest in around five deals and more than ten deals in rare scenarios at any given time. So, you're starting with odds of 100 to 1 against, which means it's critical that you do your homework from the start since they are inundated with unsolicited calls from businesses requesting contributions. They tend to disregard most uninvited approaches.

The ideal moment to start generating traction with an investor is before you need the cash, and the greatest approach to do so is to establish a rapport with them first. Rarely is it feasible. Try to obtain a warm introduction from someone they know, like, and trust, such as a coworker, an entrepreneur, a lawyer, or an accountant, someone who has regular contact with them and will advise you to go see 'X' since he has an excellent possibility and will make room for you. **One word of caution:** This is a crucial warning since you may damage your company if you ignore it. If you don't look, ensure the investors haven't already invested in a firm that competes with yours; they'll be thrilled if you stop by and tell them about your plans and corporate secrets. They won't invest in you because they'll have a conflict of interest with their fund. They're always eager to learn anything they can about you. As a result, you must identify your competition. And it would be best if you double-checked that the investor hasn't invested in a similar or close competitor. Then, you must ensure that you are well-prepared since this is your one opportunity.

First impressions are crucial, so you must be well-prepared and present your speech professionally. This implies having a succinct elevator pitch to describe what you're doing and creating a very effective investor deck and presentation. Remember, the race isn't over until it's finished. So you'll need much patience to see it through. It's also worth going through the procedure carefully because you need to be sure you're a good match. It would be best if you also comprehended that they will be extremely cautious about where they invest their money. It may take several weeks for you to meet with them in person. You'll still have to talk and present with their financial partners. After that, they'll provide you with a term sheet to negotiate. They'll be conducting due diligence on you. You'll need to put the paperwork together and look at it, in a broad sense, six months ahead of time to ensure that you have enough time on your horizon for this procedure because if you don't have enough time, you'll either need to obtain funding alternatives or delay the process. Also, don't forget that the process can be time-consuming. And, of course, keep in mind that there are no guarantees.

However, I want to remind you that we are looking at a very close business partner for five years. It is critical that you're the right fit for one another because if you're not compatible with each other and fall out after they've invested, you'll likely depart the firm. They won't go away. So, be prepared and choose your partners carefully so that you can get some assistance in locating the ideal investor for your company. Please write to me at Umran@onecallbusinesssolutions.com if you have any other questions.

21. Is Private Equity the Best Alternative for Your Firm?

It may seem odd to ask whether Private Equity is the best investment option for you in a book about Private Equity. However, examining this question has merit. Before deciding which Private Equity fund is appropriate for you, think about whether Private Equity is the best answer to your financial need. You can now choose various methods for funding your company, assuming you're a young, growing firm seeking to raise money. You bootstrap, which means you don't obtain any external capital and do it all internally generated or through your resources. You might apply for a loan from a bank, possibly from an entrepreneurship loan. It may be a venture debt provider, but it is still Debt rather than Equity. You might pursue an angel investor. You may look at venture capital rather than Private Equity or growth equity, among other things. Consider family offices or IPOs. Those are the types of things you could explore.

However, you may assess these alternatives by asking yourself a few key questions. Hopefully, this will assist you in determining where you indeed are and want to be.

So the first question is:

- Do you want to sell more than half of your business, i.e., surrender control?

If your answer to the above question is "Yes," the two finest choices for you would be Private Equity or a Family office. If the answer to that is "No," i.e., you wish to maintain control and only sell a portion of your business, you have three alternatives: Bootstrapping, Going to a lender, Angel investors, Venture Capital Growth, Equity Financing, or going for an IPO. These do not aim to acquire a majority stake in a company.

The following section is about the activity level of the investor you're searching for.

- Do you want someone to assist you with the operation and management of your business? Or even worse, to constantly watch over your shoulder to ensure you're doing what you claim and producing the milestone results you promised?

If the answer is "Yes," Venture Capital Growth and Private Equity are the alternatives. If you're looking for a passive investor, the best option is to bootstrap, get a Loan, or look for a passive angel investor. Now, let's assume you're looking in the long term and that you want someone who'll be there for a long time. Private Equity typically has a three to five-year investment cycle. On the other hand, family offices can stay in for a lengthy period.

In the case of Private Equity and Venture Capital, exit strategies frequently include an IPO or sale to a strategic acquirer. This is often within three to five years after investing in a company. However, you've become a public firm after the IPO and are still on the market. That is the extent of the alternatives. If you're looking for a short-term investor, angel investors are more than happy to take a short-term view. At times, Venture Capital is short-term, and Growth Equity and Private Equity investors will accept it under certain circumstances. Positions where they can see a short-term exit as long as they believe the exit strategy has an upside.

If you're a startup with pre-revenue, pre-profit, or positive cash flow, and if you have less than $1 Million in revenue or profit, then Angel Investors, Venture Capital (VC), or Growth Equity are the way to go. However, if you're looking for expansion and scale at a more mature organization with positive cash flow and better prospects, then a Bank Lender, Growth Capital, Equity Investment, Private Equity funding, or Family Office is the way to go.

These are the sorts of investment alternatives available to you right now. Above all, be sure that your source of funds, whether it's a bank account or some other type of investment, has the power and capacity to invest. They don't have to go to someone else for money, and they can decide. This also indicates that you're dealing with the right level of individuals within the business, especially if it's an institutional firm like Venture Capital or Private Equity funds.

So, those two questions in the background are crucial to ask. Is Private Equity the kind of investment that your company needs right now? Hopefully, this will provide you with some criteria to use when asking that question.

22. Checklist for Selecting a Private Equity Fund

Please scan the QR or use link to get the checklist (https://tinyurl.com/PE-Screening).

Let's spend around two minutes going through the checklist to understand better. I want to provide you with some structure for your company so you may use and adapt it as needed. The First factor to consider is the **Phase of the Business Cycle you are currently** in.

- Are you at the ideation phase?
- Do you have a product that's still in development?
- Do you have a proof of concept? Are you seeking product proof to demonstrate that your solution is effective?
- At what point in your Startup's lifespan are you seeking your first consumer, which is proof of customer demand that someone wants to buy what you've created?
- Are you interested in sales growth?

The Second factor to consider is: **Can you Identify More than One Client?** You might not be profitable, but at the very least, enough cash flows into your company to become self-sustaining. Then, you enter the Launch phase and, hopefully, the Expansion Phase. Depending on which of those categories best describes your company, you may now match the stage of your business growth to the types of enterprises that PE agencies claim they finance.

Next, consider the financing round. These are known as Seed (Angel – Investment), Series A, B, and C. There are other elements, such as pre-IPO secondary, when one Private Equity firm purchases a company previously owned by another. Turnarounds, MBOs or Special situations, Distressed circumstances, Development financing, Capital investment, Mezzanine finance, Venture debt.

The amount of money you need to invest will come directly from the institution, usually via a Bank or a Mezzanine fund. So it would be best if you verified that the categorization of your transaction fits that of the firms you're considering.

However, before you get too caught up in the technical details of sector investing, consider that a new Morningstar study has found three primary ways to invest in it. Do they not just invest in your Industry but also in your Sector and Sub-subsector? Businesses have become more specialized. For example, if you're in a relatively niche industry, you must locate a company that matches your business model. Make sure there aren't any existing rivals in this portfolio as well. This is significant because they will still eagerly accept a meeting with you and do their best to learn as much about your company as possible since they want to utilize it for their own. So you don't want to get caught in the bear trap. You should be sure that the businesses you're talking with haven't invested in anything similar to yours since they won't invest, but they'll happily pick your brains.

Geographic restrictions are also critical because certain businesses have them. You'll be wasting your time if you're in the wrong location. Sure, you can screen it easily but do so before you start. What are their current workplace locations? It's critical to maintain proximity to your company in order to manage your connection effectively. Zoom cannot do everything for you. You must visit them. They need to show up at board meetings. They should make introductions for you if they can. Suppose you're discussing anything to do with the UK in an attempt to open a conversation with a San Francisco-based investor. In that case, you've probably made a mistake. I've provided a checklist (https://tinyurl.com/PE-Screening), it will assist you in making an educated selection concerning the kinds of Private Equity firms you should research and talk to.

Section 5: How Do Private Equity Firms Find Deals?

23. Funding Transactions in Venture Capital and Private Equity: What They Are and How They Work

Let's start by discussing the many sorts of funding options that are accessible, including Venture Capital and Private Equity investment. Private Equity and Venture Capital financing depend on a Company's Stage of Development. In a nutshell, <u>Venture Capital invests in the Early Phases of a business's development. In contrast, Private Equity firms invest in the Latter Stages.</u> Seed Capital, Startup Finance, and First Stage of Series Finance are the three components of Early-Stage funding.

The Beginning - Seed Finance (Scenario): You're essentially an Entrepreneur. You have a product or a service to sell, but you lack the funding to get it up and running. So you'll need some seed money. Of course, you can try and bootstrap it. You may have funds tucked away. You could get a customer to pay you for your idea's development. You'll need to find cash for your vision to become a product. Most entrepreneurs get these funds from friends and relatives or angel investors, with the amounts we're talking about typically ranging from 15,000 to 250,000 dollars.

The process of obtaining Startup Capital is the next stage. But first, we must go through several steps to turn it into a product we can sell to our initial client. So this entails a greater investment, but it's typically less than $1 million. This stage is typically when the entrepreneur exceeds the "Friends and family financial capacity." However, Angel investors will put money into startups at this stage. Early-stage venture capitalists are coming earlier and earlier in the funding process, albeit with significantly more risk, who would most often examine deals of this kind.

Series - A funding is market financing, evidenced by the fact that angel investors invest. You've developed a product, and you want to scale it up so that it may be offered to multiple consumers. So, during this development phase, you'll need to scale up. At this stage, your company will still be cash-negative. The average amount of money we're raising is $1 million to $10 million. Now, don't be put off by the notion of one-round funding. What often happens is that each stage of successive growth, before a firm becomes huge, will result in waves of investment over time. To make things less complicated, the nomenclature for rounds has been updated. So Series - A is first, followed by Series - B.

We're now entering the realm of Private Equity as a result of how many funding rounds you'll need in second-stage growth finance. You may now have many buyers. It might sell a variety of items. It has the potential to operate in several markets and is very likely to be cash-positive. You'll need much money to grow the firm – rarely less than five million dollars. The objective is to expand your firm as much as possible to make it substantial.

Bridge financing is often a type of last-ditch financing to take a firm to an initial public offering (IPO) and Acquisition finance to assist your company in acquiring a rival, which is another method to expand faster.

You have Management buyout or Leverage financing in a situation like this, but it's not usually for a growing business; instead, it's for an established firm seeking to break away from its original investors. It's essential to talk about exits to complete the cycle. Investors will want to cash out and make their money at some point, even if you've got them on board. These are the most common methods by which this will be possible. The first is an initial public offering, in which the firm goes on the stock market, and investors are allowed to sell their shares. The buyback procedure entails that staff from the corporation purchase other investors' holdings.

In most cases, management will want to close out one or two, some early-stage investors and angel investors. This is a method for them to get their money back, a trade sale, often a preferred alternative to an IPO, where another big competitor company acquires your firm, and the investors get their cash that way.

More recently, and particularly in the past decade or so, you've seen other businesses acquire other Private Equity firms, swallowing up the original Private Equity and Venture Capital investors. These are referred to as Secondary sales or Second buyouts. Instead of being marketed to a trade investor, it has been purchased by another financial investor. This has given you an idea of how transactions are funded in VC and PE funds. These are the kinds of financing that you'll hear about. You can now see how they're connected to the bigger picture.

24. What Features Should a Potential Buyout Target Have?

Let's now look at what makes a suitable Buyout target company. So, for those looking to work for a PE firm, this will help you learn more about the type of businesses that PE firms are looking to target. Unlike Venture Capital firms, which focus on finding investment opportunities that 10X or will reach a Billion-Dollar Valuation (Unicorn Status), Private Equity transactions concentrate more on developing and expanding mature enterprises.

The PE Investment Criterion is focused on the following:

- The First factor to consider when evaluating a business is its Market Leadership and Long-term competitive advantage. This, again, is straight out of the Michael Porter playbook. If you're an MBA student, read everything you can find about Michael Porter and Competitive Advantage because we were reading it. Many of these are barriers to entry, switching costs, and customer adoption difficulties. These include strong customer relationships, power over suppliers, and other similar factors. That is why it's difficult for others to compete against it. It's also critical for firms already in a dominant position in the market to remain strong so that they may compete and advance. What you don't want as a PE company is to buy the second or third place in the market and then have to put much money into taking over market dominance.

- The Second factor is for you to have a Concrete Growth Plan with "Choices," I'm emphasizing here the term "Options." You want to be able to diversify your approach and not rely on just one strategy for development and growth. Product launches, new clients, potential new markets, and improved sales to existing firms and customers are all opportunities. That's the simplest solution. After you've done this, sell more to your existing client base. Up or downstream marketing extensions or acquisitions, as well as any other options that provide the potential to develop the firm without requiring a lot of money, without necessitating a large investment, is an evergreen strategy.

Also, rather than waiting for these opportunities, seize them by making appropriate investments backed by a solid implementation game plan. Your business needs to have a consistent, repeatable cash flow. Now, businesses that generate recurring cash flow from subscriptions, software as a service, or other software-as-a-service offerings are much more appealing. The cash flow should be checked to ensure that it is adequate for the financing structure and that those banks and other lenders are willing to grant you the borrowing and leverage you require in the transaction. The cash flow must also cover both interest and capital repayment obligations. You also want the company's cash flows to be consistent and non-cyclical.

If you want a low-capital investment business, you don't want to waste money on maintenance or replacement costs for worn-out assets. Private Equity firms, on the other hand, are less willing to pay high valuations for capital-intensive businesses. Positive long-term trends attract investors who don't want to buy into a sunset industry. The most effective way to think about this is the company's life cycle, in which you have a hill-type form they wish to buy on the upswing. They don't want to be caught on the downward slope. So, they're looking for ways to do well by taking advantage of progress in various markets and sectors, such as change, digitalization, and automation.

- The Third and Critical Factor is Having a Competent Management Team: What investors depend on when making a purchase, especially if it's taking over a division of a larger firm, is having someone on the inside. Of course, the deal is completed between the business's principles and the Private Equity firm; they acquire the company. After the acquisition is complete, they will give their loyalty to the buyout team instead of their old firm. If there are any secrets in the house, they will expect to discover them. You don't want to have any vacancies on your team. You'll want to make sure the team has covered all of the necessary topics and that they have the strength within this group to continue with the buyout plan. The deal's success is contingent on the implementation of this plan. Suppose they have to replace key managers at any time during the contract. In that case, it's a precarious prospect for a Private Equity concern.

Suppose the business has been undermanaged, mismanaged, or neglected for some time. In that case, numerous opportunities for value-add and financial engineering may exist. There are many things a firm can do to improve its operations if it's sleep-deprived, has a lot of useless assets, or is overstaffed. I was even party to a deal with a PE firm and discovered that the company had a corporate jet on the books. You're probably right; it didn't take long for them to be bought. I've also seen offers where the corporate headquarters turned out to be brimming with valuable art that had not been included in the balance sheet, and there was no representation of it on the company's value. Commercial real estate deals, such as retail purchases and leasebacks, may lower infrastructure expenses and operational efficiencies while simultaneously optimizing pricing. Diversification of customer bases and expansion are all possible. These are all situations in which the company may step in and conduct business to improve the deal's profits.

It's far more difficult to discover the ideal company at the perfect time. Many Frogs, on the other hand, are out there, as well as relatively few Princes. Deal activity is low, but the number of PE firms updating opportunities on a regular basis has increased. So, they impose stringent criteria on themselves to ensure they discover something that interests them if they go through enough soil. After all, they only need 10 to 15 transactions for each fund over a 10-year period. With that in mind, I hope it gives you an idea of the types of firms that PE firms seek when looking for feasible buyout targets. It's not rocket science. It's simply common sense. After you've utilized this criterion in the context above to evaluate possible opportunities, it's much simpler to spot those who don't fit and get down to a shortlist, which you can thoroughly investigate.

25. Screening for Private Equity Transactions

How do Private Equity firms evaluate potential investments? I'm attempting to introduce you to the intricacies of Private Equity firms and companies seeking financing. This will give you a better sense of the dynamics and the criteria everyone is looking at to see how transactions fit together. There are many elements to this scene.

The starting point always comes down to a deep understanding of the industry. Having a thorough grasp of the sector's components is a necessary first step. Let's consider "Software" and "Technology" for this exercise. You can find a variety of software firms, and you may notice that there are several huge, concentrated sectors with many competitors (CRM for example). Then, there are a few more specialized sectors, such as Cybersecurity.

Although you may appear to be in "Technology," you will discover that "Tech" has a multitude of Subcategories. If you delve further into each of these software categories, you'll find that they all have their own subcategories. So, it demonstrates how complicated the situation may be.

When it comes to your understanding of the sector, you must have a good grasp of not only who the firms are but also what their history is because you need to know whether they're Public Companies, Privately Owned, Venture Capital, or Private Equity-backed subsidiary of a Larger Company, Foreign-Owned Businesses, or Early-Stage Disruptors. The following are just a few clarifications and classifications to consider since it all depends on whether you're an equity investor or a company seeking targets. It would help if you were sure that you comprehend your place in this hierarchy because even at any one moment in the market, many complicated factors are at play.

Suppose you look at the typical "Technology" space in the UK, London, for example. In that case, there's much activity going on at any given moment. So, US software firms are always looking for cross-border collaborations, typically targeting some of the top 500 companies. You have European software firms interested in cross-border partnerships in the United Kingdom and those focused on the top 500 businesses. These are substantial cross-border transactions. Venture Capital and Private Equity firms seek opportunities, including secondary and tertiary transactions. These can be for the top 100 businesses, or you may have to look at the top 100 VC firms to get an idea of who these players are.

You'll also have to deal with Indian or Asian software firms attempting cross-border partnerships in the United Kingdom. These may be profitable, but they're a small handful. Then, you may contract with British domestic technology companies that are attempting to consolidate their own market. So, all these varied factors compete for business in the market. When you reach a bargain, there are still numerous obstacles to overcome, and then comes the financial difficulties, one of the most significant. However, there are many occasions when finances are tight. You must analyze every arrangement thoroughly. You need to understand the cash flow, balance sheet, and profit and loss statement. You must first comprehend the company's cash flow and breakeven points, as well as the business's funding requirements and agreement. And for earlier-stage companies, you need to know how much money they have and how long it will last at their burn rate. So, there are a lot of different terms and financial aspects to the transaction that you'll need to comprehend.

What's the best way to improve your geo-targeting? Let's take a look at geography. From the perspective of the firm, geography is crucial since it determines where its clients are. However, it is vital from an investor's viewpoint because it influences where their money goes.

In general, the earlier stage, the deal, and the investors' desire to be as near to businesses as possible are all good indicators of how close they are willing to get. It also implies that you could start with the Geographical region when it comes to putting a deal together and locating investors.

Investors and firms must be aware of the company model in order to avoid making costly mistakes, so you need to know how they make money.

- What is the company's inclination towards intellectual property or technology?
- What is their cost structure?
- Do they have a clear competitive advantage?
- Are they a specialist in their field?
- Do they have a distinct selling proposition or sound like the ones you've heard before?
- What are the company's main focuses and goals?
- Why there's an expectation that it'll outsmart its competition in marketing management?

Quality Management is, without a doubt, essential. You should consider their expertise.

- Do they have a track record of negotiating contracts?
- Do they have relationships with folks in the industry and in the finance sector?

This is especially critical to any Buyout agreement. <u>Financiers will almost always tell you that they are not putting money into the company they're investing in the Management team.</u> There are several difficulties to consider and comprehend when dealing with owners and founders, for example:

- How old are they?
- What are their price expectations?
- Is the 3D affecting them? (Death, divorce, and illness)
- Which are frequent triggers of deals?
- Is there a problem with Successor Planning or Succession?

When it comes to interacting with company owners, you must be extremely sensitive about their personal situations. In the previous chapters, we discussed the various kinds of deals.

Finally, in your screening, keep an open mind. There is also a time cost to the complicated process of screening and approaching objectives, discussing, arranging meetings, offering terms, negotiating them, and going through due diligence before signing them. These are all things to keep in mind when it comes to comprehending the intricacy of Private Equity.

26. Funnel for Investing in Private Equity

Let's look at a deal funnel for a Private Equity firm now. Let's say you've just started your first year on the job and are still new to the firm. You will have some staff, so it's essential to know how many deals you'll look at and how many deals you'll do. If you're a business needing financing, you should first reverse the process and consider how good your chances might be for receiving capital from a particular firm, given their deal funnel.

Private Equity firms are seeking a needle in a haystack, to put it another way. They're usually inundated with deal possibilities. They want to be flooded with deal possibilities and see as many deals as possible. It's known as being in the deal flow. If you're not seeing any of the beautiful offers, it's because you're not seeing all of them. You won't see some of the fantastic deals if you don't view all of them. So they're eager to see as many deals as possible, but they want to do so in an efficient manner. So they don't want to sit down and talk with you. They want to get it done in a straightforward style. And I'm going to teach you how to do it that way.

However, remember that if a Private Equity company does 10 to 20 transactions throughout its existence, it must put money into the first five years. So, if you invest ten deals in five years, that's two transactions each year. That isn't much, but much labor must be completed to get to those two transactions conducted. In a given year, they'll go through anything from 300 to 500 deal summaries, potential deal transactions, and one or two pages in a quick way and throw away the majority of them. They may choose from that stack to evaluate 100 books. Bear in mind that books can be a 20-page sales presentation or a 50-page comprehensive business plan with the time, effort, and thought required. And they don't want to devote too much time to it. They are required to do so. They'll be in negotiations with several experts and management teams from 20 to 30 companies. So they're getting into the nitty-gritty of 300-500 deals and down to 20.

Off the 20, they'll aim to get rid of at least half and then sign the letter of intent. Because they've already signed the LOI, they don't want to do all of that due diligence work because they'll have lawyers and accountants and don't want to pay for that. They'll try to shift the burden to the other side but seldom succeed. They'll be concentrating on signing LOIs with only agreements that you're serious about. They only want to sign one to four agreements yearly, with four being the most optimistic scenario. So, as you can see, this funnel gradually narrows from three to 500 at the top to one to four at the bottom over time. And that's just during a single year. Because of this, the most efficient thing they can do for them is to eliminate a lousy arrangement swiftly. If a potential deal doesn't check every one of their boxes, they'll kill it and move on to the next transaction.

When you're presenting and putting together your pitch to Private Equity firms, you must make sure that you address each of their concerns. Don't forget that each company has its own quirks, so you'll need to adapt your approach in order for them to take your offer seriously. As a result, knowing what makes up a Private Equity firm's deal is essential. You need to realize that you're at the top of a very long funnel, with only one layer separating you from the bottom. If you want to go from top to bottom, you'll need to put in a lot of time and effort. You've got to do your homework and get your pitch perfect if you want to go from bottom to top.

Section 6: Deal Structuring for Private Equity Funds

27. Capital Structure of a Private Equity Acquisition

Let's jump right in and discuss the Capital Structure of a Private Equity Buyout.

Capital Structure of a Private Equity Buyout

Assets	
	Bank Debt (20% - 60%)
	High Yield (0% - 15%)
	Mezzanine (0% - 15%)
	Equity (15% - 50%)

While every transaction is unique, a Private Equity deal's Capital Structure can be outlined in a Framework. Each transaction employs "Debt," i.e., Private Equity Buyouts are highly "Leveraged." Debt boosts investment returns while increasing the risk of financial failure for the Capital Structure. The four most important features of a financing structure are Bank Debt, High-yield Debt, Mezzanine or Quasi-Equity, and Equity.

Now, each component has a distinct yield or return. The deal is divided into separate pyramids of priorities, with senior to junior. The most senior loan, however, has the lowest return, and the most junior loan offers the best return. Let's start with a bank or senior Debt. This typically has a 3% to 8% return and a floating coupon. This is usually priced at around 100 basis points above LIBOR or the going bank rate in the country. For example, suppose a vehicle loan has an interest rate of 5% and the bank debt is 1%. In that case, each percentage point represents 0.01% or one percent. Don't forget that a basis point is one percentage point of one percent of whatever has the lowest financing cost. It also has the lowest default risk because it gets its money back first since it is the most senior component of the financing structure. It relies on the business's earnings and typically has yearly interest and principal payments, as well as covenants to safeguard lenders and the company's assets.

Let's look at a few more essential elements. The firm's cash flows come first, but its outstanding Debt has the highest priority. That's something you should bear in mind. The primary goal of the floating rate, interest rate, and capital repayments is to repay the loan in 5 to 10 years. The loan agreement will also contain covenants, which ensure the company fulfills appropriate standards for the lenders to ensure that the business can service and repay its Debt at all times. A few methods include the "Interest Coverage Ratio," which specifies minimal interest coverage and a maximum debt-to-cash flow ratio, ensuring that the cash flow can always pay off the loan installments.

On the other hand, High-Yield Debt has a higher interest rate, typically 8 percent to 14 percent, but it's a fixed-rate loan. It does have less restrictive covenants and ranks below senior Debt. Still, it may also result in a second charge over the assets. Early-year prepayment penalties are typically imposed to ensure that high-yield debt investors know they'll receive their high yield for at least a set period. High-yield Debt is also known as subordinated Debt because it is subordinate to senior debts. When it's in the form of a Bond, it's also known as High-yield Bond or Junk Bond. It's frequently interest-only. As a result, you are paid back the capital at the conclusion of the term. It ranks above Equity, but it lags behind Senior Debt.

There may also be an option to pay a Premium, which allows the company at a later stage in the transaction to refinance the structure. The Deal structure also includes the rights to call the Debt, i.e., repay it early by paying a premium. This caveat comes in handy when you can borrow money at a low interest rate for an extended period, thus saving you money over the life of your loan.

A small proportion of "Bridge finance" is also included in the "Deal Structure." This is typically resulting in a profit of 15 to 20 percent. In some cases, instruments that include Warrants may have pledges attached, giving the holder of the warrant the opportunity to invest in Equity. It protects the instrument holder, provides downside protection for Debt, and offers equity upside potential. Mezzanine or quasi Equity may also include payments made in paper rather than cash. In this case, the debt instrument may consist of convertibles, debentures, and the benefit of convertible Debt, which puts it above common Equity in a downturn scenario. However, in the best-case scenario, it may convert to Equity and rank above a significant portion when everything goes smoothly. If it's turned into Stock, it'll be ranked the same as the Equity. So, it's a form of structure that grants Private Equity Investors an advantage in the event of a decline, protects them from liability, and enables them to profit from the general Equity.

Common Stock or Equity is the fourth component, typically delivering a 20% to 40% return. In theory, the potential is limitless. Equity generally has the highest risk and, as a result, the highest return. So, in the case of a failure, when the firm is liquidated, assets must pay off all other creditors before Equity can be paid. The riskiest type of company is a Private Equity fund, which has not yet raised any capital. One option for raising funds is to sell pieces of the business in exchange for cash. The most junior creditors, contingent lenders, generally finance buyouts with Debt and quasi-loans from banks and specialized fund investors. They're aiming to put a restricted sum of money into the deal. Then, the company's profits and success over time will enable them to repay their remaining high-yield Debt and bank debt to those investors, leaving them with only the Equity in the company's full value. There is a brief explanation of the capital structure of an equity buyout. It's much more complicated than this, but that is the broad overview structure with the four essential components.

28. What are Equity and Common Stock, and what do they represent?

Let's clarify what "Equity" is and how it differs from "Common Stock." <u>Common Stock is the security that gives owners' rights to a firm and allows them to elect the board of directors and vote at meetings.</u> In the United Kingdom, they are known as Ordinary Shares rather than Preferred Stocks, and dividends are paid to common stockholders instead of preferred stockholders. Companies frequently issue Debt, Preferred Stock, and Common Stock in addition to Bonds. There is Stockholders' Equity on a firm's Balance Sheet, which is the value of the common Stock.

Here's a look at Apple's balance sheet.

Apple Inc.

CONDENSED CONSOLIDATED STATEMENTS OF OPERATIONS (Unaudited)
(In millions, except number of shares which are reflected in thousands and per share amounts)

	Three Months Ended		Six Months Ended	
	March 27, 2021	March 28, 2020	March 27, 2021	March 28, 2020
Net sales:				
Products	$ 72,683	$ 44,965	$ 168,361	$ 124,069
Services	16,901	13,348	32,662	26,063
Total net sales [1]	89,584	58,313	201,023	150,132
Cost of sales:				
Products	46,447	31,321	108,577	83,396
Services	5,058	4,622	10,039	9,149
Total cost of sales	51,505	35,943	118,616	92,545
Gross margin	38,079	22,370	82,407	57,587
Operating expenses:				
Research and development	5,262	4,565	10,425	9,016
Selling, general and administrative	5,314	4,952	10,945	10,149
Total operating expenses	10,576	9,517	21,370	19,165
Operating income	27,503	12,853	61,037	38,422
Other income/(expense), net	508	282	553	631
Income before provision for income taxes	28,011	13,135	61,590	39,053
Provision for income taxes	4,381	1,886	9,205	5,568
Net income	$ 23,630	$ 11,249	$ 52,385	$ 33,485
Earnings per share:				
Basic	$ 1.41	$ 0.64	$ 3.11	$ 1.91
Diluted	$ 1.40	$ 0.64	$ 3.08	$ 1.89
Shares used in computing earnings per share:				
Basic	16,753,476	17,440,402	16,844,298	17,550,281
Diluted	16,929,157	17,618,765	17,021,423	17,718,591
[1] Net sales by reportable segment:				
Americas	$ 34,306	$ 25,473	$ 80,616	$ 66,840
Europe	22,264	14,294	49,570	37,567
Greater China	17,728	9,455	39,041	23,033
Japan	7,742	5,206	16,027	11,429
Rest of Asia Pacific	7,544	3,885	15,769	11,263
Total net sales	$ 89,584	$ 58,313	$ 201,023	$ 150,132
[1] Net sales by category:				
iPhone	$ 47,938	$ 28,962	$ 113,535	$ 84,919
Mac	9,102	5,351	17,777	12,511
iPad	7,807	4,368	16,242	10,345
Wearables, Home and Accessories	7,836	6,284	20,807	16,294
Services	16,901	13,348	32,662	26,063
Total net sales	$ 89,584	$ 58,313	$ 201,023	$ 150,132

Apple Inc.

CONDENSED CONSOLIDATED BALANCE SHEETS (Unaudited)

(In millions, except number of shares which are reflected in thousands and par value)

	March 27, 2021	September 26, 2020
ASSETS:		
Current assets:		
Cash and cash equivalents	$ 38,466	$ 38,016
Marketable securities	31,368	52,927
Accounts receivable, net	18,503	16,120
Inventories	5,219	4,061
Vendor non-trade receivables	14,533	21,325
Other current assets	13,376	11,264
Total current assets	121,465	143,713
Non-current assets:		
Marketable securities	134,539	100,887
Property, plant and equipment, net	37,815	36,766
Other non-current assets	43,339	42,522
Total non-current assets	215,693	180,175
Total assets	$ 337,158	$ 323,888
LIABILITIES AND SHAREHOLDERS' EQUITY:		
Current liabilities:		
Accounts payable	$ 40,127	$ 42,296
Other current liabilities	45,660	42,684
Deferred revenue	7,595	6,643
Commercial paper	5,000	4,996
Term debt	8,003	8,773
Total current liabilities	106,385	105,392
Non-current liabilities:		
Term debt	108,642	98,667
Other non-current liabilities	52,953	54,490
Total non-current liabilities	161,595	153,157
Total liabilities	267,980	258,549
Commitments and contingencies		
Shareholders' equity:		
Common stock and additional paid-in capital, $0.00001 par value: 50,400,000 shares authorized; 16,686,305 and 16,976,763 shares issued and outstanding, respectively	54,203	50,779
Retained earnings	15,261	14,966
Accumulated other comprehensive income/(loss)	(286)	(406)
Total shareholders' equity	69,178	65,339
Total liabilities and shareholders' equity	$ 337,158	$ 323,888

Shareholders' equity:		
Common stock and additional paid-in capital, $0.00001 par value: 50,400,000 shares authorized; 16,686,305 and 16,976,763 shares issued and outstanding, respectively	54,203	50,779
Retained earnings	15,261	14,966
Accumulated other comprehensive income/(loss)	(286)	(406)
Total shareholders' equity	69,178	65,339
Total liabilities and shareholders' equity	$ 337,158	$ 323,888

Essentially, the value of a firm's common Stock is determined by subtracting its Total Liabilities from its Assets. The Balance Sheet shows that we have Assets, Liabilities, and Shareholders' Equity. <u>Shareholders' Equity is the result of subtracting Liabilities from Assets.</u> When people invest in a firm, the company's cumulative retained earnings are added to over time from its profits. Investors prefer Convertible Preferred Stock to Ordinary Stock in a Private Equity firm. Convertible Preferred Stock protects them against losses and gives those rights and protections relative to earlier investors. That's Equity and Common Stock, in a nutshell, the foundation for any firm's capital structure. It's even more critical when you're looking at Private Equity deals.

29. Preferred Stock in Private Equity Transactions

Preferred Stock is a difficult topic in Private Equity agreements. In this chapter, we'll hit on some of the key features. Preferred Stock has many more benefits than simply giving equity ownership rights in a company. In the UK, Preference Shares are known as Proxy Voting Rights. In any Private Equity transaction, a Preferred Stock is often created for the Lead Investors and the Private Equity firms.

Always be prepared to review the rights' details connected with a Preferred Stock. However, this is not legal advice; remember that preferred stocks come with many complexities. "Preferred" was coined because this Stock has additional rights and privileges over common stockholders. Let's go through a few of them in greater detail.

There are Four types of Preferred Stock (*Every Private Equity transaction is unique, and you should always study the specifics of the rights in depth*).

- **Cumulative Preferred Stock**: This applies to most "Preferred Stocks." In other words, if a dividend is withheld or not paid, it builds up in arrears. It must be reimbursed before the Common Stockholders are entitled to any subsequent dividends. This is a feature of Public Company Preferred Stocks rather than Private Equity. This allows the issuer, or firm, to redeem Stock at a price and time in the future.

In a Corporate Acquisition, the Preference Stock is utilized as a tool to provide the acquirer greater rights and control. Also, they don't want to be on the receiving end of a call option for that Stock. Convertibility entails the point at which investors can exchange their shares for cash. The timing of the price is established in Preferred stock terms, such as during a company's liquidation or after a merger when the conversion happens.

As we'll discuss later, the holders of preferred Stock may wish to re-enter common Stock to take advantage of the transaction participating. The dividends, on the other hand, may now be guaranteed. There might be a pre-determined rate linked to it. In any case, dividends will be calculated according to a formula. They may contain an extra dividend compared to common Stock. You should also read through the fine print, especially if you're entering a long-term agreement or financing. You must understand that Private Equity transactions utilize preferential rates to protect and manage their investment in a firm. They have extensive and physical rights attached to them. As a result, they enjoy the right to information.

Typically, it includes financial information, capitalization table data, budgets, and inspection rights. This implies that they have access to enter businesses and get comprehensive access to corporate facilities and records. Everything they wish to liquidate. In other words, if everything doesn't work out and the firm is liquidated, any cash that remains after paying all creditors and debtholders goes to preferred stockholders first. They're the first to receive a return of funds.

- **Dilution Protections:** I've mentioned this as a broad principle, but Private Equity yields on preferred Stock are typically convertible into Common Stock at the option of the preferred stockholder. When a firm undergoes a sale or merger, stockholders who owned preferred Stock before the transaction convert to common Equity and participate in it. You must also look at the specifics. Preferred stock investors benefit from this because it protects them against dilution, which means that their percentage interest in the firm is decreased due to future financials. It's also important to consider the small aspects. This is why capitalization tables may get quite convoluted.

- **Priority Voting:** The shareholder's agreement allows shareholders to elect one or more directors to the company's board. Given that they will ensure their concerns are addressed on the Board, Priority Voting rights help them exercise these rights. They might also have (in some cases) "Veto Power" over significant corporate decisions intended to safeguard their own position.

In the event of a Buyout, Private Equity firms have the advantage of paying out more dividends than public stockholders. Dividends are usually not paid in PE transactions, and accumulation of dividends is allowed before common stockholders receive their full dividend payment. Most of the time, they are built up. However, because the bonds are rolled up and incorporated into the Equity owed to preferred stockholders before being able to be refunded by common stockholders, some of your money may have already been returned.

Preferred Stocks are the main type of Stock that an entity issues. It's a difficult subject. Remember that Private Equity firms employ these frequently to protect their investment compared to common stockholders. When it comes to Private Equity transactions, you must study the specifics of the Preferred Stock rights to grasp the situation.

30. Preference Paid to Preferred Stockholders on Liquidation of the Company

Let us now discuss Preferred Stock Liquidation preferences. A Liquidation Preference is a right preferred stockholders hold for priority payments in the event of a firm's liquidation. The liquidation preference affects how the liquidation process is split between preferred and common stockholders since it influences how property is distributed to them.

A "Liquidation Event" is when the business owner closes operations and sells off its assets. The failure and closure of a company might be referred to as liquidation. If that's the case, the company's assets are used to repay creditors and debt holders. Then, it's divided among preferred and common stockholders. Liquidation preferences, on the other hand, can imply the sale or consolidation of a firm. Finally, the liquidation preferences are utilized to distribute the sale proceeds.

On the other hand, the Ordinary liquidation preference states that Preference stockholders will get their money back or a multiple of their money before common stockholders. Put differently, the multipliers may be one or more, implying they get their money back. It's conceivable that it will be 1.5X, 2X, or 3X the amount they invest. This means they can recover a multiple of their investment before common stockholders receive any return.

The Preference for liquidating your account may also include the payment of any outstanding or accrued dividends and other payments. When these preferred shares are combined, and no dividend is paid, the accumulated dividend must be repaid before common stock investors receive cash.

Preferred Stock is divided into two categories:
- **Preferred Stock**: This has a fixed dividend.

And
- **Participating Preferred Stock:** This implies that the preference shareholders are paid their anticipated dividends. However, they contribute to the pool of cash from which common stockholders are compensated. And in most situations, this happens when the preferred shares convert to common stocks. As Preferred Stock, they are paid once. Their Stock is restricted, conversion plans are developed so that their Stock converts, and then they rejoin the common stockholders' pool of money for a second time. So you need to be conscious of it, too.

Now, there's a circumstance where that participation has a maximum amount, and this implies that preferred stockholders can only get so much money before common stockholders have to contribute (either by participating on a shared basis or their own). It also implies that common stockholders are more likely to receive compensation from the transaction. In a worst-case scenario, liquidation options might reduce the cash available to preferred stockholders by leaving no money in the pool. For the most part, common stockholders are entrepreneurs and founders of a company. Thus, in some cases, the "Investors" may get nothing.

This is why determining a liquidation preference in Private Equity deals is important. It's a crucial topic. You must go and read the fine print on liquidation preferences.

31. More Rights for Private Equity Investors

Let's review the "Rights" of Private Equity Investors a little more in-depth. It's critical for you to understand how they impact deal structuring. We've already reviewed some distinctions between stock classes and particularly preferred stockholders' rights. But I'd like to go through some more legal conditions you may encounter in Private Equity transactions, sometimes called "Rights." You should be aware that several financing rounds, such as A, B, and C, lead to different classifications of Preferred Stock. In other words, each new class of investors will receive a different cocktail of rights. Future investors will always try to protect themselves ahead of current investors through these rights. The term downside protection is another issue to discuss, and it's a catchall phrase, but you must know what it implies.

The term "Hedging" refers to the terms that investors negotiate into these stock categories to lower and eliminate any potential losses or downside risks. This is the point of most Private Equity transactions, which investors are eager to fund. Then, they spend the bulk of their time speculating on the potential bad outcomes and constructing rights and systems to prevent themselves from those outcomes. Each class of shares has its own set of privileges. These rights may not be altered without the consent of that class of shareholders. They're also known as **Class rights** because they represent a right for a certain group. **Pre-emptive** rights are also crucial. **The Right of the First Offer** means an investor can participate in future or subsequent investment rounds to maintain their stake in a firm.
The Right of First Refusal is the polar opposite. It concerns situations when one existing stockholder wants to sell his shares, and the other can purchase them on any terms established with external buyers or investors. You must be conscious of those two and the difference between them.

We've previously discussed **Information Rights**, and, in essence, stockholders have the right to financial information from the firm, as well as access to an assortment of data about corporate records and physical access to offices. However, you should be aware that I am emphasizing, mainly if you are a class holder, that you have the legal right to obtain this information about the firm. The Directors are unable to suspend these privileges. The term **Registration Rights** refers to the right to register a new name. **Illiquidity** is inherent in Private Equity investments. A right of **First-Class Registration** allows the stockholders to force a company to register its shares with the SEC after a period of time. This enables the Stock to be sold in an IPO, at which point investors can sell what is presently an illiquid asset. <u>The right of Veto over certain major corporate decisions, even if an investor does not control a majority of the equity in the firm, is known as a Negative Control.</u> This covers anything from dividends to capital investments to borrowing and any changes in company activity.

Materiality is a term that many estate planning attorneys are unfamiliar with. It's an essential concept in all these agreements, meaning what is vital, significant, or necessary. It also tries to ensure that when any of these provisions are activated, there is a check for significance before applying an event or term condition in the agreement because it must be something significant or material rather than something insignificant. Small things in and of themselves may trigger a lot of tension, turmoil, and fights among employees. If you apply a materiality test, you can reduce these incidents; however, there are frequent debates about what is essential and what isn't.

These are just a handful of the rights you'll discover in Private Equity transactions. You'll encounter them in many business deals, but you need to know their existence and how they work.

32. Examining Capital Structures in Private Equity Transactions

Let's get into the nitty-gritty of capital structures in Private Equity deals. Leveraged Buyouts employ "Debt" to boost returns for the "Equity." This is at the heart of a Leveraged Buyout. The Capital structure, on the other hand, is not a set formula. It's adaptable, negotiated, and assessed but still crucial to the transaction's success.

In any transaction, the best capital structure is one of the most important elements to evaluate. These factors include the expense of debt, its flexibility, and what you can do if things go wrong in any deal scenario. There are several blocks to a Capital structure: bank or senior debt, junior debt or Mezzanine, quasi-equity, and common equity. The returns on these tiers account for their cost, risk, and seniority in the event of a default or liquidation.

So there's a tradeoff. The greater the seniority, the less risk, the lower the coupon, and the cheaper it is. The total debt amount might be as high as 10%, but most are between 4% and 8%. Senior debt is generally within a range of 4% to 8%. Junior Debt runs from 8 to 14% in interest rates. Quasi-equity is 15 to 20% of the total capital fund.

So, while formulating a capital structure, you must first determine the total cash flow from the firm available to service the debt. Now, this is what you do with your LBO model. You make a Cash flow forecast. This is the prediction you underuse to support your analysis of a capital structure, which is what we will talk about today. You must ensure that your capital structure has adequate headroom, which is why standards such as senior debt, set covenants, and thresholds for things like the level of debt and interest payment coverage are important.

You'll need to start by restricting what you put into your model. Senior debt, commonly around 60% of the structure, has the lowest cost. In the event of default, it is first in line to get its money back. You must consider this when computing quarterly and annual interest rates and principal repayments. It also has a floating rate interest rate. So, if interest rates in the market rise, your capital costs will have to be adjusted for, but you also have some leeway to raise this. So if you're several years down the line, you've already paid off part of the loan and want to recap, you can return to the sea, the bank, and argue that you are a trustworthy lender.

Do you have any additional cash, please? The junior or high-yield debt, which can account for 30% of the structure, is a distinct species. It's a fixed-rate loan. There are no amortization payments on it. Because the investors want to connect their returns for various years generally, there are early repayment penalties. It's important not to overlook this point. It's all about adaptability, but it's a less flexible instrument with fewer restrictive covenants. It also ranks behind the senior debt in terms of priority. It may have a second lien on the company's assets, secured by the senior debt.

Leverage can help you make much higher returns on equity than senior debt. However, the more leverage there is, the greater the danger of collapse. Equity is typically about 15% of a Capital structure. You won't find it in every transaction. It could be a convertible share or some proof, or it may have some warrants. In other words, a convertible note is an instrument that allows for converting the assets into equity immediately after purchase. It also includes warrants, which give equity upside in certain situations, such as an exit event. So you're giving away more money but also using another piece to leverage the returns to equity even higher. And the question you need to ask yourself is <u>how aggressive you want your capital structure to be.</u>

The Common Equity, which is 20% to 50% of the structure, is at the bottom rank in the event of a default. But, in comparison with other funds, it offers investors a higher return because they are paid back first and then invested to generate more cash flow. In conclusion, remember that what remains must be divided between equity and debt (or profits). This is fantastic, but it's all about evaluation and balance. Too much leverage might destroy a deal in a recession or when things go wrong. Too little leverage, on the other hand, implies that additional money will have to be put up by the equity investors. They also take on more risk because, as their return increases, their multiples will be lower if they put in more money. It's all about the risk-return tradeoff in the end.

Your LBO model aids in developing downside scenarios and stress-testing various capital structures. However, it is also about bargaining with debt collectors to obtain the lowest price and the most flexibility on their terms. Since most of this information is already out there (particularly with banks and high-yield funds), most conditions are standard, and there isn't enough wiggle room for bargaining. That's one area where you can explore how to evaluate your capital structure once you've completed a Private Equity transaction. It isn't set in stone. It's not a template exercise. You'll need to consider it with your Leveraged Buyout model for each Deal to see what it can withstand without overleveraging, and without causing financial distress in the event of a downturn.

Section 7: Value Creation and Metrics

33. How Do Private Equity Firms Make Money?

Let's now examine how Private Equity firms make money.

How to Private Equity Firms Make Money?

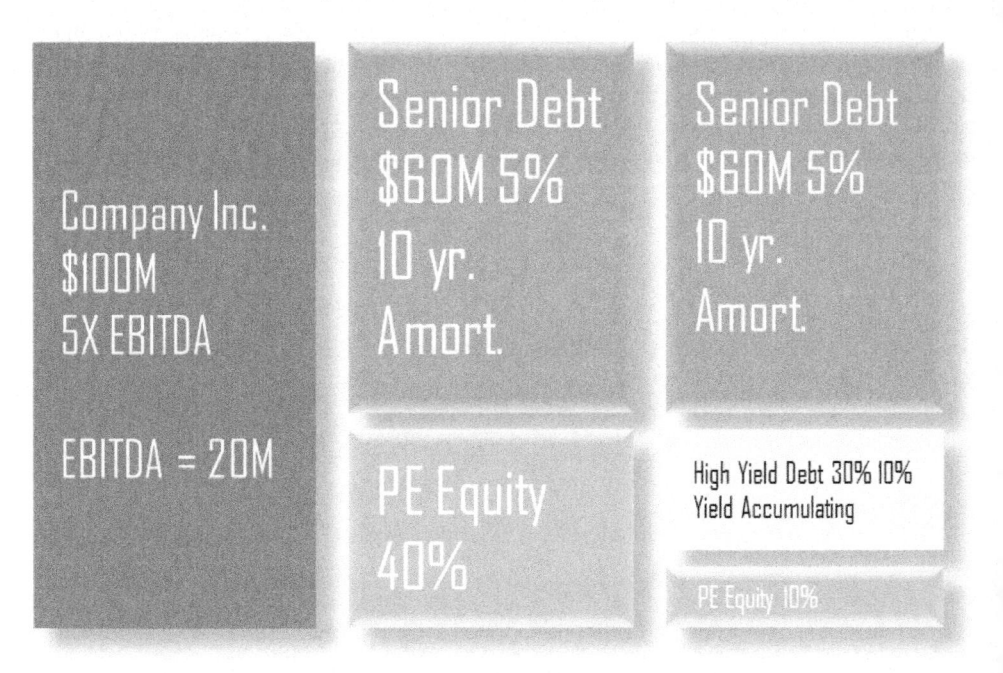

| Company Inc. $100M 5X EBITDA EBITDA = 20M | Senior Debt $60M 5% 10 yr. Amort. PE Equity 40% | Senior Debt $60M 5% 10 yr. Amort. High Yield Debt 30% 10% Yield Accumulating PE Equity 10% |

You will learn how Private Equity firms utilize Deal Structure, Timeliness, and Three Key Principles to achieve transaction profits.

1. Leverage
2. Arbitrage
3. Expansion

Deal returns are often more complex than this. However, if you grasp these three principles, you'll be good at comprehending how Private Equity companies produce returns on investments. To make a hypothetical transaction more concrete, I'll describe how a Private Equity firm acquires Company Inc. for $100 million and pays 5X EBITDA. So, EBITDA is $20 Million, and the issue now is to figure out what the firm can do with this cash flow to generate a return. EBITDA is used as a proxy for Cash flow in this example.

The First step is to use "Leverage" in the transaction. As a result, you have the term Leveraged Buyout (LBO). The total consideration is $100 Million. They're playing 5X EBITDA but don't want to put any of their own money into it. So, the first thing they do is borrow money secured by the company's assets and cash flow to compensate for part of the payment. In this scenario, they took out a 60 Million Dollar loan with a 5% return. This will be 200 basis points over LIBOR or whatever the current rate is in practice. Let's say it's 5% and has a 10-year amortization, which means the capital is repaid over ten years of the agreement. This gives the Private Equity firm control of 60 Million Dollars (40 percent) of the transaction. They're paying a 5% interest rate and must make 10% yearly payments. The interest cost is $3 million per year, and the amortization period is $6 million per year. This would be paid quarterly rather than annually.

You'll need to add some High-yield debt or Mezzanine to boost returns. Let's simplify by discussing High-Yield Debt alone (*the Mezzanine almost always includes equity warrants and other complications*). Let's assume that a Private Equity firm has raised $30 million in High-yield Debt at 10%. In reality, it might be up to 15%. The high-yield debt investors are looking for a certain return on their investment. There's no way to pay this back for three years. They are not paid, but interest is accrued. As a result, it has no effect on EBITDA or quarterly cash flow. It may be a five-year term loan, for example. After five years, it will either have to be repaid or recapitalized. There's no debt amortization, though, until then. It all adds up at the end.

So you've already paid 30% of the cash agreement, though it's expensive; nevertheless, it's much less than equity. So the company has 10% of the contract. As a result, they've invested 10 Million dollars for a 100 Million Dollar transaction. They've got 60 Million Dollars in bank obligations and 30 Million Dollars of high-yield debt. However, they still have 11 Million Dollars in free cash flow. In this example, we're talking about 11 Million Dollars of cash flow. Using the cash flow statement, we'd do all this in a typical assessment. The Free Cash Flow must be huge enough to meet the bank covenants, particularly interest coverage.

So after five years, the Senior debt has been reduced to 36 Million Dollars. The interest on the High-Yield Debt has been rolled up. As a result, the outstanding balance is now at 45 Million Dollars. Debt has increased from 54 Million to 81 Million since then. Assuming no change in valuation, the PE's equity is now worth 19 Million Dollars, or 1.9X the invested capital. That doesn't seem like a good return right now, but keep reading because it improves.

What about those earnings? What about all of that cash flow? Because a surplus has been accumulating for years, we did not account for it. Assuming you're making more money than you need for your company's growth, the excess cash will either grow, be reinvested in the firm, or be paid out as dividends. Let's assume that it builds up in the company and the 19 Million of equity we presently have. We also possess 58 Million Dollars in cash, which technically belongs to the equity. Suppose you pay off a debt with it.

In that case, the equity value has increased to 77 Million, seven times the original investment (7X). That is, after all, only assuming a company's original value at five times EBITDA of 100 Million. So, we haven't altered the EBITDA valuation in the least. The equity value has already risen to 77 Million. Of course, any tax concerns have been completely ignored until now. So, a word on taxes since profits are taxable and dividends are taxable when paid. The shareholders must pay tax on dividends and income tax on dividends. Interest and debt amortization are not taxed because they take advantage of a tax shelter. In other words, you can make these payments before determining your tax liability at the profit-before-tax level. Any tax paid in an equity deal like this is simply a waste of money to the agreement.

You have to now comply with all of your legal responsibilities. And we're not talking about tax evasion; instead, we're discussing how to structure a transaction to get the best outcomes for the Deal while minimizing taxes as much as feasible. You want this money working for you rather than leaking away to the IRS. I emphasize once again that it must be lawful and genuine. Leverage is working well for us, and I'm assuming we repay at the end of the five-year term since it's ended.

In practice, it's likely that the senior debt will be recapitalized, i.e., they'll put additional debt into the firm to pay off some or all of the high-yield debt. Much of it has to do with taxes, and it's also about maintaining the company's financial structure as leveraged and efficient as possible. Don't forget that interest tax interest expenses are deductible in taxes. As a result, leveraging the situation has worked effectively. The equity returns have improved dramatically, but we haven't taken advantage of this fantastic aspect of development and compounding growth yet.

What if we presume that we invest 5 million dollars of the cash flow into the business each year, which grows by 10 percent? Don't forget you add five million dollars of value to the transaction for every additional one million dollars in EBITDA. It's also reasonable to anticipate that firms, if successful, will develop organically over time. However, I'm not comfortable with taking things for granted. So, the organic growth and investment in the company are giving me a 10 percent return, 10 percent growth of the firm, and a 10% increase in EBITDA. So, with $55 million a year in new investment and an EBITDA growth of 10%, we'll see our EBITDA climb to 32.2 million at the end of year five, as opposed to 20 million previously. As a result, if you maintain the EBITDA multiple five times, the company's equity value is now $161 million. However, we also have cash in year five of $67 million. Before we pay off any debt, we must first deduct $81 million in debt. This leaves an equity value of $147 million. As a result, the firm returned to its original value. Our return to equity has increased fourteen point seven times (14.7X), but we still have work to do. Although the return on investment (ROI) has increased by two times, we haven't considered the Arbitrage advantages.

Now, PE firms dislike paying too much into a contract and would argue that many of the failed transactions occurred because they overpaid going in. They seek to acquire things at a low price. It's the real keystone of a good deal. In the interest of fairness, we should also acknowledge that if they put less money into their business in the long run, it will protect them considerably on the downside. Let's assume they can sell the business at seven times EBITDA (7X). This isn't expensive, but I'm not going to argue that it's a four or three-times entrance point; however, let's suppose they can sell the company for five times EBITDA. They're getting an arbitrage. They're receiving a benefit not just on the company's activities but also on the price they purchase. They buy low and sell high, making money on the difference between the two multiples. At the end of year five, EBITDA was 32 million. It rises to 35 million after year six. Suppose the firm successfully contends for a seven times historical or prospective EBITDA multiple. In that case, they're increasing the transaction's value by 64 to 70 million dollars.

Because of the leverage in the agreement, the senior bank debt and high yield are paid off. The remaining money, "Equity," is replenished. This goes to show how "Growth," "Leverage," and "Arbitrage" have benefited the PE firm. Let me highlight that the example presented above was very simplistic. It's not exhaustive, but it provides a few points that complicate things, which you must consider moving forward.

Working capital is the first of these. Working capital is the money you'll require to conduct business. Now, as enterprises expand, they need greater working capital. This, in turn, will have reduced the cash reserve. But remember, when firms are sold, they adjust working capital.

Businesses will try to remove as much of the working capital cash as possible to make this a problem relevant to the entry and exit points of any deal. There's no longer any such thing as an investor who doesn't understand how the market works. Working capital is straightforward: you have to figure out the working capital and ensure it has just enough flowing in and out, affecting cash flow, and any free cash that remains after paying bills goes into the seller's pocket. There's no debate about the assets on the balance sheet, any investment they'll need, or even the ability to sell and lease back some of these assets, as it did in many of the large retail deals that were Leveraged Buyouts in the early 2000s.

There's much fun to be had with it. The PE Company may opt to recapitalize the whole Deal and take a significant dividend, continuing the arrangement for another five years. It has happened before. So, there are many strategies to do it, and you may continue increasing the gains. The PE firm is completely risk-free at that point. They've recouped all their investment and gotten a substantial return, yet they still own the firm.

Planning for taxes is a crucial component of any transaction, and we haven't discussed it because I'm not a tax expert. And I don't want to hopscotch in that minefield, either. There's no debate about the senior management or workers' role and compensation in an option pool. So, there is no discussion about sweat equity, which also forms part of the equity slice. However, it simply implies that the cake is sliced differently. There's no word of any previous investors who might have a minor stake. The return to equity is the end of this. Of course, it's true. The PE firm would not have invested the full ten million dollars. That would have necessitated involvement from other investors as well. In practice, the equity capitalization table is almost always more complicated. Cash flow, now the most important indicator, hasn't been discussed in detail. This is why it's critical to have a cash flow model in place. You'll want a profit instead of a counterbalance sheet or cash flow; they all work together to form one entity.

I've used EBITDA as a stand-in for cash flow. To keep it simple, I'll say this: I haven't focused on the risk element of the transaction alone. Remember, greater the leverage, the higher the risk. The biggest hazard is to be run by the equity investors, who are the most minor in recapping liquidation profits if everything goes south. In other words, your equity may be reduced if the Deal does not pan out. And I've only shown you one side of the equation; there's another. In practice, many deal details, structuring, and terms are focused on insulating the PE firm from risk. They come with many privileges. It's all about protecting yourself from the downside. I haven't talked about internal rates of return IRR yet. This is a time-based measure of success that I don't want to try to describe right now. I've concentrated on cash returns and multiples because they're much simpler and easier to comprehend as a measure of deal success.

To summarize, **Arbitrage** is a mechanism that PE companies employ. They buy low and sell high. They utilize **Leverage** by borrowing and leveraging other people's money. However, they face financial risk and rely on growth over time to improve their return on investment. These strengthening factors working together allow the PE companies to make money. So, you've seen now how complicated issues in real life are.

This is a straightforward upside-only example, but it does, I hope, illustrate and explain how Private Equity firms generate returns from the deals they undertake using these three key variables.

34. How Do PE Firms Generate Value for a Portfolio Company?

How do Private Equity firms add value to a portfolio company, and how does the process of Private Equity investment work in general? It's not only about entering low and exiting high when generating value for a portfolio company. There's much work to be done in the middle. And it's this labor that provides investors with major gains. Private Equity Investment Firms and Management Teams of Portfolio Companies work closely together.

They always sit on at least one board seat and attend ten monthly and quarterly meetings. As a result, they're smack in the middle of the business's day-to-day operations. They expect monthly reports and always go through them meticulously, asking questions and challenging management about them. Now, as they attempt to avoid becoming involved in the firm's day-to-day operations, they do want to produce "Alpha" returns for the company and themselves. *The **Alpha** return is a term used to describe how much effort an investment manager makes to add value, as opposed to the **Beta** return, defined by market conditions.*

The types of things PE firms evaluate are Financial, Strategic, and Operational plans. They also bring their skills and expertise to expand the firm since their interests are focused on the same goal. They have extensive Connections, to begin with. These connections aren't limited to the financial sector any longer. Depending on the PE firm's specialization, they're also present in industries such as Oil and Gas, Manufacturing, and Retail.

PE firm
s are constantly in contact with many firms; they get to know many individuals and meet several people at the top level. That puts them in a fantastic spot to make introductions and gain access to specialists, financiers, and other top-level advisors whom they can subsequently formally or informally meet as management team members. If you think about it, they've already run a company; they spend much time working and looking at numerous firms, sitting down with management, discussing how their enterprises are operated and what they're doing with them. You can always look back to see what you've learned and how you may apply it to your current situation. That is especially true of Private Equity executives, who are more hands-on than other investors.

Of course, there are also excellent practice skills to be learned, which they may have picked up while working for another company. And their current management at their investment firm may not possess that knowledge. They can bring those things and teach the management what they should be doing and what they could be doing to improve the quality and running of the business. Now, the things for which they may make improvements are rather basic. For example, Sales optimization, Pricing approaches, and Cost savings are ways to improve. Of course, in certain situations (such as Six Sigma), they can replace or modify some or all of the management team. They can also select the appointment and removal of company Directors. <u>Transformational management is a big term, but it refers to significant adjustments in the way a company does things that must be made to improve its performance.</u>

A Private Equity firm's and its executives' external vantage point, when they join a company, can assist in identifying overlooked issues and driving them through implementation. They can drive the optimization of inefficiencies and business practices and improve the supply chain and distribution channels. If you have the insight, The value chain is up for examination and potential improvement. Of course, employee numbers are never taken for granted. They may require increased or redistributed staff. It's important to note that acquisitions necessitate a certain level of knowledge. However, Private Equity firms frequently have people on a team.

Given that they are constantly purchasing and selling businesses, it's clear that they have personnel with similar expertise. It's unusual for them not to. Private Equity firms can identify and execute acquisitions with great speed. They can also aid in the integration of organizations. Various PE funds set up platforms from their investing firms and go out and acquire and bundle several businesses to build a market-leading firm. These variables all aid in the quickening of growth, increasing economies of scale, and eventually profitability. There is more to it than meets the eye regarding Exit timing and value optimization. Private Equity companies are, without a doubt, experts at maximizing sales values.

They're also notorious for buying and selling at the top of markets. They set up firms with a strong track record as part of their plan. They optimize working capital to ensure they don't have too much cash on hand. They're going for the highest possible exit sales multiples by putting the company in the best possible position to benefit from them. Furthermore, there's the issue of assessing market timing.

All these elements come together to ensure you get the best possible purchase price. Although financial engineering may appear to be a black art, it is not difficult once you understand what you're doing. We've already seen that buyout firms have complicated financial structures to establish the power necessary to produce equity returns. Private Equity firms are constantly attempting to improve the financial structure of their companies for it to contribute to stock growth and value appreciation for investors. Those are a few ideas on how Private Equity firms add value to a portfolio company. They are not passive investors. They're going there to work with management teams to ensure everyone gets the greatest return possible.

Section 8: The Deal Process in Private Equity

35. The Deal Process in a Nutshell - Part 1

Let's walk through the "Private Equity Deal Process" process from start to finish in greater depth. This topic is divided into five chapters. Senior Executives in Private Equity Firms are responsible for Deal Origination. This occurs when they notice deals that are good for them, either because they made the connection themselves or because it was recommended to them by their network. The procedure to start is lengthy. It involves a lot of analysis, networking, thorough study, cold calling, meetings, and legwork. In essence, Private Equity firms are constantly on the lookout for opportunities. That isn't to say they don't do any deals. We've already seen how their funnel works and the amount of screening they must go through to get to the point where they're ready to begin seriously discussing a potential transaction.

In-house deals are called Proprietary agreements when they're sourced. These differ from acquisitions brought in by a financial institution, such as an Investment bank, which is selling a firm. The Private Equity buyer must compete against Strategic or Industry buyers in a competitive situation. In most cases, this is done using a controlled auction conducted by the Investment bank. However, it places Private Equity firms in a position where they must compete rather than take part in proprietary transactions, which are generally more one-to-one.

When it comes to competitive processes, the situation is now reversed. Because large organizations have a shortage of opportunities to work on, the deals they can do are few and far between. Smaller Private Equity firms are more likely to get investment banks arranging it for them. They'll likely be able to identify private businesses where they can organize a bilateral negotiation without the influence of external competition.

Let's detail the Major Stages of a Private Equity transaction. When a Private Equity firm and a Business or an Investment Bank have reached an agreement on a non-disclosure agreement, the transaction's starting point is determined. There's also the Investment Bank, which provides a Confidential Memorandum to the Private Equity firm. There's an exchange of information between the PE firm and the Company. If an Investment Bank handles a sale, they will generally release a one- or two-pager summarizing the firm and opportunity. This is often known as a "Teaser." The PE firm then signs a non-disclosure agreement known as an NDA. The NDA has been signed, but it's been signed directly with the firm and is in return for access to a limited amount of confidential information sufficient for the PE firm to make an initial assessment of the opportunity.

The first step is the Preliminary Due Diligence and Management Presentations, which the PE firm will begin with. It will conduct initial Due Diligence on the firm by checking everything supplied. Then, the team will draw up a Strategic Business Plan. *The Business Plan includes identifying Key Competitors and Markets, Assessing Industry Trends, Forecasting Future Demand for Products and Services, Building Competitive Advantages through Cost-Cutting Measures (or Price Increases), Raising Cash by Issuing Bonds or Equity to Investors at market rates to finance growth via debt.* They'll have to start inquiries into debt, such as bank loans and other financings, to get a sense of the terms and scale of the debt that might be available. They'll start thinking about the transaction's financial aspect and produce an initial due diligence information request list.

In a Bank-led process, the Management team would then give a presentation about the Company and themselves to a select few buyers, which hopefully will include the Private Equity Investment team if the firm is still in the transaction. The presentation to the Private Equity firm's first investment committee meeting follows. The Private Equity investing team will then prepare and deliver an initial presentation to the Private Equity Firm's Investment Committee. A two-to-three-page overview of the opportunity generally supports this presentation. They're attempting to secure preliminary approval for the Deal to proceed. The conclusion of the meeting will include a green light for an initial first round, which is usually around the same range as values. The Deal may progress if the investment committee gives its approval.

The Private Equity firm now pays for the Due diligence costs. Limited Partners do not support them. Private Equity firms are extremely cautious about how they spend their cash since they can't get it back. This is the beginning of the Private Equity deal process.

36. The Deal Process in Private Equity- Part 2

We're in Part Two of our look at the "Private Equity Deal Process." We'll be looking at how Private Equity Deals Operate and go back to where the firm will submit a Non-Binding Letter of Intent and a First-round Offer in the Sale Process. *A Letter of Intent (LOI) is a non-binding document that outlines the broad lines on which a Private Equity firm may propose to make a deal.* The "Purchase Price" is included, but instead of an actual number, there will be a reference to the Purchase Price. They'll be able to Quote, Explain, and Clarify the proposed Capital Structure and some of the fundamental assumptions on which their offer is based. If those assumptions change, the terms of their offer may need to change for them to complete the key due diligence activities and when they want to make a binding offer. They'll summarize their experience and background in a few paragraphs and explain why they believe they're an excellent investment for the firm. They'll describe their objectives towards management and staff and the permissions they'll require internally and externally to complete the Deal.

The Investment Bank and the Selling firm will evaluate whether or not they want to accept the PE firm's offer based on what's in the Letter of intent, which is non-binding, as well as any additional competing bids that may be on the table.

What is the difference between a Letter of Intent and a Non-Binding Agreement? The Letter of intent contains a binding clause that usually includes confidentiality. So, on both sides, it confirms that the procedure is confidential.

Assuming that the Selling Business accepts the Private Equity firm's Non-binding Letter of intent, we proceed to a Stage of due diligence and the "Data Room." Due diligence is an ongoing process that gets more complicated with time. The firm has only provided a restricted quantity of sensitive data to a select number of prospective purchasers. The Company doesn't want any important data in many people's hands. As a result, you wind up with a funnel process where the deeper you go, the more information you acquire.

In the 1980s and 1990s, a data room was precisely that: A large chamber filled with binders and stacks of paper to which access was strictly limited. You'd go in there with a whole group of people and go through all the documents, but you wouldn't be able to take anything home with you. Nowadays, all data rooms are virtually organized (As simple as a "Dropbox or G-Drive" folder with assigned permissions), allowing you to access them or not. It is still handled confidentially. The data is still restricted, but you don't have to go to a room. The Company preparing it didn't have to duplicate everything physically and put it into binders, which was time-consuming and expensive. The Private Equity firm goes through the sensitive data, which has been provided in great detail. It will include any additional due diligence questions requested by the Private Equity firm.

Due diligence is a time-consuming process. The data room contains much information. They cover everything from financial to legal services to employees and anything else you can imagine about the Company. The Data Room data is then analyzed, and a series of calls are set up between the PE firm, the bank's management, and the other consultants to address queries that may arise from the data analysis. At this point, third-party specialists may be hired to give reports on the goods, markets, competition, and other concerns deemed vital to the transaction. Later in the book, we'll learn more about them.

As a result, the Private Equity firms will provide us with a financial operating model. And what they do is construct a thorough business running model from the data room information. This allows them to study how they expect the Company to do overtime. It's a very bottom-up process. It includes the finest details of products and services, key drivers, pricing, and everything else they may put into it. They make their basic assumptions. They include their Leverage, financial structure, and forecast deal outcomes and returns on a five-to-ten-year time horizon.

The PE firm arrived in the Data Room, completed its investigation, and gathered all the information. They've asked questions and created an operating model based on their responses. They're progressing with the transaction right now. In the following chapter, we'll continue this step-by-step approach and learn more about the "Initial Investment Memorandum."

37. Private Equity Deal Process - Part 3

After entering the data room, they complete their investigation and gather all the information. The PE firm had prepared a Corporate Operating Model based on their responses. In Part 3, the Private Equity firm will focus on preparing the **Initial Investment Memorandum**. This is the final, expanded version of the original paper submitted to the investment committee. They've now transformed this into a 30-40 page document for evaluation by the investment committee in the next stage of their transaction appraisal.

Let's go through the content of the **Initial Investment Memorandum** since it's an important document.

The Initial Investment Memorandum begins with a General Description of the firm. This may sound like a business plan in many sections until we conclude. You have the firm's History, the description of Goods and Services, Customers, Suppliers, Competitors, Corporate Structure, and the Management Team. You'll get an overview of the Market and the Industry, Key Market Growth Drivers and Trends, Company Position, and Company Positioning compared to Competitors.

In this example, we'll look at a Stock Financing Agreement that's made between a Corporation and a sponsoring Private Equity firm. This book's "Due Diligence" Section will cover Risks and Due Diligence. There will be a list of potential Company and Industry Hazards and any issues that have yet to be addressed. There will also be a chapter on Valuation, which will discuss comparable firms' valuations. They'll compare it to prior M&A transactions in the same Sector to see if it's comparable. A Discounted Cash Flow (DCF) analysis will result from the Operating Model and a discussion of Leveraged Buyout Model Assumptions and Results. There will be a discussion of the Exit strategies, as they always want to think about how they'll get out of a transaction before they enter it. There will be a summary of possible Exits and a discussion of likely timelines. The document closes with recommendations and a project plan.

The budget for the transaction is covered in the document. This requires the Investment Committee's approval, and they will be seeking permission to hire any third-party consultants for any due diligence reports covering commercial, financial, or legal concerns that they anticipate will be required for the Deal.

At this stage, the Private Equity firm's investment team will begin discussions with prospective lenders, including senior debt and mezze or junior debt. They'll usually contact a small handful of lenders for this. But, due to their existing connections, PE firms are more likely to have working relationships with banks they already know, who know them, and how they operate. This group of banks will be quite small, and they'll want to have a little rivalry to ensure they get the greatest terms for the debt they're bringing into the agreement.

In terms of diligence, the cost is kept to a minimum because it's expensive and always left as late as feasible in a transaction until they reach critical milestones. It's a trade-off, though, between how much time and money you spend on due diligence. We've given the case to the investment committee with the preliminary information memorandum. We've received approval for the transaction and begun our talks with banks and third-party consultants about potential debt arrangements and additional due diligence reports that we may require in-depth from the third-party experts. Part 4 will examine how such arrangements function in the real World.

38. Private Equity Deal Process - Part 4

We're now at the point where we're doing our Final Due Diligence in preparation for submitting a Binding Offer. The transaction has yet to receive approval from the Private Equity Firms Investment Committee. However, we enter the closing phase of our investigation, during which time we finalize the binding offer preparation. This is a phase of prime focus for any PE firm. They attempt to gain information by phone and ask questions because they need more knowledge about any outstanding deal-related details to complete their due diligence.

Third-party advisors will be performing commercial, financial, and legal due diligence before providing their reports to the board. These reports can be 30 to 60 pages long. They're also fantastic sources of information and key insights. These reports significantly impact the business's future because they educate the Private Equity firm a great deal. The PE firm's legal advisors are now beginning to draft the sale and purchase agreements and other documentation, which will be the initial draft. Private Equity firms generally write the seller purchase agreement. ***The Seller's team never provides legal advice. There's a valuable lesson in this. He who controls the Pen wields the Sword.***

When the legal team creates this document, everything is slanted towards the benefit of the PE Company. However, when the contract is completed, it's difficult for company legal advisors to restore a fair balance to the document. And this is one of the art forms of M&A legal negotiations. They'll also be dealing with the PE firm and advancing the negotiations with prospective debt providers on the amount and terms of the debt to start finalizing the structure they want for the transaction. Furthermore, the banks that provide this credit will have their diligence concerns, which will need to be addressed and answered by the Private Equity investment team. They'll now update the Information Memorandum, and they'll go through final Investment Committee Approval.

After the due diligence, the investment committee must be updated, and the most crucial deal issues and terms must be represented and confirmed. This is completed in a document known as the Final Investment Memorandum, essentially a finalized, up-to-date version of the preliminary investment memorandum. The deal team presents, creates, and delivers this. The document contains a detailed view of the transaction, which includes a conclusion-specific revenue and deal structure. The entire document, as well as the whole agreement, is now subject to the consideration of the investment committee.

Once authorized, the investment team submits their final, binding offer for the firm, which includes terms of the bank financing they intend to utilize in conjunction with the debt they want to acquire. The Buyer will want to sign a final purchase agreement and an updated, but not completed, sale and purchase agreement for further discussion. The Private Equity firm could proceed exclusively to finalize legal documentation and any outstanding concerns before signing the Deal if it is chosen in a competitive bid. An exclusivity period is set to overcome the barrier if it's a company-to-company transaction.

Finally, we've reached the point where the Private Equity firm has received clearance from the investment committee. A binding offer letter has been submitted and accepted by the selling firm and their investment banking consultants, as all due diligence has been completed.

39. Private Equity Deal Process - Part 5

The Ending and Concluding Stages of the Deal Process are covered in this chapter. We've completed all the paperwork once the agreement has been reached and signed. A joint press release is issued, but the transaction hasn't closed. After that, the Buyer and Seller must collaborate to complete the transaction. This could take anywhere from a few weeks to a year or more. It all depends on the size and intricacy of the transaction, as well as whether the target firm is Public and whether any regulatory or other permission is required. There are just too many variables to go into detail about the possible outcomes. However, <u>you must recognize the difference between entering into a contract and finalizing one</u>. There are always things to do between signing and closing to ensure it gets over the finish line.

Close attention must be paid to the Management Equity and the Option Pool. Depending on circumstances, the management's equity interest in the new Deal might need to be agreed upon and negotiated. They may already have a prior equity position rolled over or be investing money in the transaction or joining the option pool. The equity position must be negotiated, and the option pool must be established and authorized.

In a Public transaction, remember that the Private Equity firm is not permitted to discuss Compensation with Management until after a Deal has been signed. The purchase price will be determined after all the closing conditions have been satisfied, including paying a portion of the debt. As part of the Closing process, we'll look at Debt financing since, before the Deal can close, the debt must be finalized and in place. This will require documentation and detailed conditions to be approved prior to signing off. The other problem is synchronizing the money flows with all the parties involved in the Deal. Suffice it to say that orchestrating a transaction's closing process is like trying to put an orchestra together. It's a challenging procedure.

It's generally led by the legal team rather than the Investment banks. However, it does take time to get right, particularly in significant transactions where Billions of dollars may be changing hands and numerous parties are involved. This is a complex logistical operation that must be completed and organized carefully.

So, at the end of the Deal, all the paperwork is completed and simultaneously signed, and we're in business. That's all there is to it. This helps you comprehend a Private Equity transaction's step-by-step procedures and structures.

Section 9: Private Equity Deal Due Diligence Processes

40. Private Equity Deal Due Diligence Processes

Due diligence is one of the most crucial aspects of any Private Equity deal. We will spend some time going through a multi-faceted due diligence process that typically takes place in Private Equity deals. <u>Due diligence confirms details of matters under consideration via investigation, audit, and review.</u> The procedure must be exceptionally well organized, structured, and detailed. You're attempting to discover whether there's anything rotten with the firm you're buying and, if so, what it is. It's comparable to purchasing a vehicle from a used car dealer. He'll most likely keep silent on the issues. You'll need to inquire yourself. Then, if he misleads you, you have a remedy. Full disclosure is expected. However, you won't receive the proper answers if you don't ask the correct questions.

Commercial due diligence is the most challenging because the management, the Selling firm, and Shareholders will all present the Company in the best light. The management is well-versed in the business. But you may not be. You also need to figure out for yourself what the truth is, especially on the business side. Due diligence is often the responsibility of specially selected advisors, such as accountants and management consultants. Legal and financial due diligence is more confirmatory in nature. Suppose the sellers give all of the information they are requested and present it with honesty and sincerity. In that case, the selling purchase agreement's recourse against them is considerably decreased. The Seller discloses under the sale and purchase agreement while deferring financial and legal judgments until later.

This Section will examine Commercial due Diligence and Financial and Legal Investigations to see which subjects and regions are addressed within the three primary topic areas. This is not an exhaustive list; you should not rely on it. If you're doing a due diligence investigation on your deals, consult with your attorneys, lawyers, and accountants and utilize their experience and knowledge. That is their duty. That's a brief overview of what due diligence is.

41. Competition and Markets - Competitive Due Diligence

We'll start our thorough Commercial due diligence analysis focusing on Competition and Markets. Commercial due diligence, in the broadest sense, embraces everything the firm does to generate revenue, earnings, and shareholder value. We'll look at the market competition, which includes the Company's value proposition, products and services, market position, historical performance, and industry and market trends.

When we talk about Competitive and Market Position, we are looking to answer two fundamental questions:

- How sustainable the Company's business model is?
- Where does the Company stand in comparison to its rivals? To do so, we must first explore the Company's Competitive advantage. We discuss items, technology, pricing, branding, distribution channels, and geographic markets.

- Is the firm a Disruptor in its Market? So you're referring to everything Michael Porter discusses in his book The Competitive Advantage. However, it is critical to consider the Company's place in its Market and its competitiveness. Michael Porter can provide you with a fantastic perspective on corporate competitiveness.
- Are there any entry restrictions for potential competitors?
- Is it difficult for businesses to compete with our own Company?
- Is there a cost to switching to a competitor's product?

Switching costs are a major influence on customer loyalty. Customers are much less likely to switch to a different product if the switching costs are high. If they're low, it'll be relatively simple for them to swap.

- Where is the Company's place in the Industry Value Chain? Is it at the value chain's top, bottom, or middle? To assess a firm's competitive position, it is critical to analyze how its competitors perform in the same category. You want to examine the past five years' industry trends and developments and attempt to forecast future changes and developments. You want to know how the Market works to better understand the Company's challenges.

Then you must look at the Firm's Major Rivals or Competitors. You want to track the Company's market share and its competitors' changes over time. The BCG Matrix (Growth-Share Matrix) is a fantastic case for doing this. The Boston Consulting Group Matrix (BCG Matrix) or the Growth-Share Matrix is a model that categorizes businesses as Stars, Cash Cows, Dogs, or Question Mark (?) based on their expansion and market share. You can apply The BCG Matrix to study any Business.

- What is the Market's Structure, and How Fragmented or How Concentrated Is It?
- What's the Penetration Rate of their Products or Services?
- What Other Solutions Exist on the Market?
- How Saturated is the Market? You also want to understand the Company and market lifecycle.
- Where is the firm you want to acquire regarding its life cycle and the market lifecycles it serves?

There's a lot to think about, but I'd like you to extract some key points and conduct further study of them. That's a brief rundown of Commercial Due diligence's Competition and Market side.

42. Sector Expansion - Large Corporations Undergoing Commercial Due Diligence

Let's move on to the firm's Development, beginning with Growth in the Sector and Industry. Due Diligence for a Company also focuses on the Market Environment and External Factors that impact it. We're looking at things like historical market growth and future market development.

- How much growth is there in the Market that the firm wishes to compete in? We also want to calculate the total addressable Market. Total Addressable Market (TAM) helps us determine how much room there is for the Company's growth and what level of industry maturity and future growth trends there are.
- What proportion of the Market does the firm control? Whether it's expanding or shrinking? And where is the firm positioned concerning these segments?

We're not looking to find what's wrong with a Company. We're looking for where the real growth potential is in a customer's products and services.

- Where are the items and services that aren't correctly positioned since the categories in which they're competing aren't growing but they might be declining? We want to know the Company's overall objective, why it was founded, and who its key customers are.
- What are the most important aspects, trends, and developments influencing the Company?
- Have there been any significant changes in the sector or industry landscape over the previous five years?
- Have there been Disruptive New Entrants?
- Is there much Consolidation in the Market?
- Is there Vertical or Horizontal Integration?
- What are the Supply and Demand Imbalances?
- Do any Regulatory or Environmental concerns exist in the Sector? These may be risks that the firm is susceptible to. Could they have an impact on the firm in the future?

That's a summary of the Industry and Sector growth factors you should challenge management on.

43. Commercial Due Diligence - Customers and Suppliers

Our objective in this chapter is to comprehend the connection between Customers and Suppliers. In addition to understanding how their interactions with clients affect each other, we want to determine how loyal and retaining our consumers are. And, of course, how reliant is the organization on its suppliers? So, it's the risk of losing your clientele. We have a hard time acquiring new consumers and the threat of having suppliers holding sway over us.

We keep coming back to Michael Porter. The Number and Concentration of consumers are crucial. I've studied transactions where a single Client was responsible for half of their Company's sales. For a Buyout agreement, this is not a realistic customer structure. Ideally, no single customer should account for more than 10% of sales. To determine the degree of concentration, look at the top 50 customers and how much they contribute to your business. It isn't very sensible to look at a few individuals.

- It's crucial to think about the length of the customer contract. How long do you keep your clients linked to a contract?
- What are the renewal levels?
- What is the proportion of contracts that renew? And, as a result, what is the churn rate in consumers?
- How difficult is keeping the same number of consumers if you have trouble keeping them happy and engaged with your brand to retain their business for another year?
- What is the value of a customer?
- What percentage of customers purchase other items from your firm?
- Can you sell additional products to your client base, which may be useful?
- Who are the key people making decisions within the client base? This is crucial.
- Do you have a long history with these consumers and many levels of connection with them?

You don't want to rely on anyone inside your firm for important client interactions with your key customers. If that one person leaves the Company, chances are they transfer to another competing business and attempt to steal them.

You must also take into account the Purchasing Psychology.
- What is the customer's buying process?
- How do they make purchasing decisions, and how can you sell to them?
- What is the typical Sales Cycle Length?

You should summarize or request that the management summarize your Company's recent Wins and Losses. *What you want to know is why they Won and why they Lost.*
- What are the underlying causes of these trends?

Let's move on to Vendors. The number of suppliers is crucial.
- We want to know how important they are and how reliant we are on them.
- What is the balance?
- How significant is the firm to that Supplier? *If they regard you as essential, there's much trust. If you're like the fiftieth customer, you have minimal influence over them.* <u>The ability to exert control over suppliers is a crucial component of a company's Competitive edge.</u>

It's important to consider the relationship's and supply contracts' lengths. Also, consider how long you remained tied to them. This will help identify if there's potential to improve the terms in your agreements. This results in greater profitability if you negotiate better terms with your suppliers.
- To what extent can you spread these items on to your customers? Will you get margin pressure if they raise their prices on you but not the costs?

So, there you have it: some thoughts on Clients and Suppliers. We're following the Michael Porter Competitive Advantage framework. It's worth emphasizing the concerns Michael Porter addresses in his books about the power of Customers and Suppliers when you're talking about due diligence concerns with the management team.

44. Commercial Due Diligence - Capital Requirements

Let's now look at the Capital requirements as part of our commercial due diligence inspection. This is critical to the success of every Company, whether it's working capital, operational expenditure, or capital expenditure. We've already established that Private Equity firms dislike highly capital-intensive businesses since this usually implies they must raise more funds, and these firms absorb cash. They don't want capital depletes. The companies that consume a large amount of money but generate lots of it are the ones in which PE Firms invest. They are focused on the cash flow to pay off the Leverage.

PE firms assess Capital expenditure. Replacement funding will be a major consideration for them. They'll want to look at expansion capital and renewal money. The capital cycle, which is apparent from the Cash flow statement, must be understood. Working capital also depends on the cyclicality of the Company. What level of visibility do you have into projected sales in the future? This is all about cash management and understanding when the money comes in. The Cost of goods sold structure is crucial to grasp, as it tells you what percentage of the total cost is paid out in fixed and variable costs. If your sales go down and you have a lot of fixed costs, you won't be able to cut those expenses. If the expenditures are variable, the Company may be able to scale back. Because of the improved efficiency, you will have fewer expenses from variable purchases. You won't suffer the same profit issues that you would otherwise. The same may be said for operational expenditures.

The bottom of the EBITDA line is where you'll see expenses from services, marketing, and other activities that don't reach the cost of goods sold. The split between fixed and variable working capital isn't often correctly understood. Consider it as the oil that keeps a car's engine running. Having a company where you manage working capital effectively is crucial.

So, one of the most important questions is: what amount of money is required for a company to operate it? Negotiations go on for weeks in terms of the working capital talks. There are also situations where Private Equity firms acquire inefficiently run enterprises and can improve operational efficiency. This results in a large amount of cash being extracted from the Company immediately on day one. It's like getting a bonus. As a result, you must comprehend the cash cycle in order to make effective use of it.

The capacity level of the firm is critical to comprehend.
- What kind of capacity does it have right now?
- Is there more sales capacity when the Company's revenue goes up?
- Is it possible to increase sales without spending much more on the Company?
- Suppose demand drops (*always thinking about "downside" protection*). How quickly can the capacity be adjusted to minimize costs and avoid losses?

This last question warrants much introspection: what would be your biggest concern in a negative scenario right now? Covid-19 was a disaster that shows how poorly prepared we are in the event of a pandemic. This Worldwide epidemic is an epic illustration of a worst-case scenario. If you're looking at today's World, you have to consider the possibility of future epidemics. You should include them in your thinking. Question the management and explore their major concerns if there is a significant downturn. Those are the few factors to consider in Capital Expenditure-related Due Diligence.

45. Commercial Due Diligence - Financial Performance

The final aspect of commercial due diligence, which we'll focus is Financial performance. The historical and future financial results are critical to the modeling and Deal's success. Your operational and Leveraged Buyout financial modeling must accurately represent the Company's future expectations. To do this, you're reliant on the firm's management; however, you want to understand how reliable their forecasts are and how true they are. You may compare the Company's historical performance to its management budgets over the last five years in order to get executives to explain why they exceeded their budgets.

- Are they very conservative, or did they accomplish a lot?
Or
- Why didn't they meet their budget expectations?
- What were the primary measures management used to assess the firm's performance?
- Did they underestimate or perform poorly? You should have a basic understanding of the major performance indicators that management utilizes to monitor company performance, and you'll need to include them in your modeling.

Don't be discouraged, but be concerned if the management isn't clear on which key performance indicators they should use. You'll need to account for organic growth in the Company over the last five years. If the firm has made a few acquisitions, you'll need to get rid of them to grasp the organic non-acquisitive growth. You need the management to describe the key growth drivers, their key assumptions in their projections for growth margins, and changes in KPI metrics. You're looking to uncover everything that's going on beneath the surface.

The final stage in aligning your predictions is comprehending the firm's threats. Consider a SWOT analysis of your assets, opportunities, challenges, and threats. And you're seeking to figure out what the dangers are.

- What are the dangers to the Company?
- Is the firm reliant on introducing new items or services?
- Are they concerned with entering new geographic areas or markets?
- Do they have a lot of customer concentration?
- Do they need to find new people to hire?
- Are they dependent on a large amount of R&D spending?

These are some of the due diligence factors that pertain to a firm's Financial success. You must be able to trust that management projections are realistic and correct to get inside the skin of the business.

46. Due Diligence in Financials

Let's look now at the subject of Due Diligence regarding Finances. Accountants will be called in to conduct financial due diligence on the Company to verify the accuracy of the financial data supplied to them. Accountants will review all of the financial information and inspect the Company's most significant sections of finance, which we shall now look at.

They want to know what the Earnings are before anything else. This implies that they want to know the Company's true level of earnings after removing non-recurring and recurring costs. This is something that you'll want to consider when evaluating the financial health of a company. The EBITDA line, in particular, is a key driver of the business's Valuation. The PE firm will use adjusted EBITDA times to arrive at a valuation. And the term "adjusted" is critical.

Some of the modifications covered are management adjustments, particularly true in private firms, company-related changes that may relate to accounting concerns, and pro forma changes that may impact the effects of acquisitions or divestitures. They also get an accurate picture of the Company's earnings and EBITDA.

Regarding debt, the Company must first understand the amount of existing debt and debt-like products within the organization. Next, these must be subtracted before the purchasers receive their sale consideration money. You don't want to pay them the entire amount of sale consideration only to discover that you'll have to reimburse a lot more debt. The Buyer will be paying it twice. As a result, commodities may include paid capital investment or equipment that has yet to be delivered. But the invoices haven't arrived yet, and it hasn't yet been recorded on the books. Deferred compensation accounts payable is a relatively clear one. Any tax-related liabilities that might be present or could arise in the future.

The second element to consider is the Normalized Working Capital. The Private Equity firm wants to ensure the Company has adequate working capital to keep operating since any deficit in this calculation will be subtracted from the sale proceeds. Due diligence must also understand the Company's financial requirements throughout the economic cycle to ensure the firm is not acquired when its working capital requirement is artificially low.

The next point is the Tax Structure. Tax Structure ensures that the Company's affairs are orderly and efficient. I'm not a tax expert, and this book isn't about tax advice. Tax law may differ from Country to Country, as well as various systems. Suffice it to say that the firm does not want to pay more tax than the law requires. The phrase legally obliged is used to emphasize their duty. And they'll go to great lengths to ensure it stays that way.

Although IT resources are not necessarily a financial issue, they influence the Company's capacity to correctly manage and report its performance. As a result, if the IT is faulty or outdated, it might jeopardize the firm's accuracy of specific financial data. It may also necessitate a significant investment to bring it up to speed. The department oversees matters connected with human resources, including payroll and all associated taxes, so there are substantial financial risks. They are likewise a liability for state and federal regulatory filings, which must be adhered to.

That is a quick rundown of financial due diligence. In reality, these are volumes and pages of specific criteria. And a comprehensive report from the accounting firm investigated the financial disparity. The complexity of the challenge is indicated by how many issues must be addressed, but at least you should have a general idea of what needs to be improved.

47. Legal Research - Legal Due Diligence

The Final aspect of Due Diligence we must examine is Legal due Diligence. This is largely a confirmation that the firm has no future liabilities, such as regulatory litigation-related or onerous contract terms. The firm must also make corporate filings, and all past and current corporate documents must be accurate. By looking into the Company's organizational structure, legal corporate structure, and business activities, a firm may learn nothing unusual or irregular about the Company's creation. They'll also need to understand the definitions and foundations of all written contracts, which include any legal agreement between you and the firm that has a material impact. There's a Materiality test for this, which significantly influences the Company's success. They must examine all previous and present material contracts to ensure no hidden issues. They're also looking at various subjects, including dates, debt arrangements, acquisitions, and other potential liabilities.

The next stage in the audit is Property, Plant, and Equipment (PP&E). This entails a comprehensive evaluation of all assets and liabilities connected with property, plant, and equipment. Operating and or capital leases are examples of liabilities. This includes all HR, Payroll, and Employment issues concerning the Management team and all employees in a business. There are also things like the terms and conditions of employment, employment contracts, any collective agreements with unions or anybody else, and the Company's compensation structure, as well as for senior management. They're worried that if they don't carve the indemnification expenses out of their health plan, which they didn't do before because it was too complicated, their liability would increase significantly. They have to carve out any possible severance payments, as these will be a liability from the Deal. Any health and retirement plans must be examined thoroughly to ensure they comply with local, state, and federal laws.

The Information Technology structure might be quite complicated, thus it will come with a large number of relevant legal agreements. All software, hardware, and maintenance contracts relating to software or hardware acquired from third parties must be investigated. The terms of any service level agreements should be reviewed, and any license agreements and their compliance should be fulfilled. So, for example, ensuring that you have licensed copies of Microsoft software is a basic step. That sort of information has to be tightly controlled. Any open legal actions related to the Company's operations, such as litigation or claims, are all examples of risks. That said, it's important to understand the nature of this case. Once again, I'm not a lawyer, and I'm not about to try and interpret this one down. Finally, of course, today's environmental issues are crucial. Environmental consequences might be extremely costly. These are only a few of the things that may result in lawsuits for your Company. They must be discovered, identified, and ensured that there is no unjustified or legal liability due to past activities. Legal due diligence is a very intricate topic and it's crucial to get it right the first time, else you could be buying a firm with a long list of obligations that will come back to haunt you later on.

Section 10: Valuation and Pricing in Transactions

48. How Do I Value a Private Company in a Private Equity Deal?

Let's discuss how to value privately held firms. If you look at Public firms, valuing them is quite simple: they have a certain number of shares outstanding and a share price. They also have a profit and loss statement (P&L) and stock. In this case, the Market Capitalization = [Number of shares in circulation] * [Share Price]. Not only that, but this data is readily available regularly. As a result, assessing the worth of Public firms is straightforward. However, this isn't the case for private businesses.

There is no Public market for the Company's common stock. As a result, their share price and financial data, including the number of common shares outstanding, may not be available to the Public. As a result, valuing private enterprises is considerably more difficult. Private Equity firms must determine the worth of their prospective investments before purchasing to ensure they are not paying too much for them. Before entering a contract, they must complete a valuation process throughout the ownership period.

General Partners and Limited Partners must be able to assess the Value of portfolio companies regularly, usually quarterly. The ability to Value a firm is critical to understanding the Portfolio's performance. Valuation also plays a significant role in "Exiting" the investments or any "Liquidation" event.

Valuation assessments are essential from the point of view of the Company Founders, Stockholders, and Advisers. These assessments help determine whether to go Public, seek investments in PE or VC firms, or figure out the worth in case they'd want to Exit.

Let's look at some of the techniques used in Valuing Private Firms. *This chapter aims to give you a glimpse into the World of Valuations.* <u>We are not looking to explore the intricacies of Company Valuations.</u>

1. **Similar Valuations:** <u>With a Similar Valuation technique, we are searching for a group of Publicly Traded Businesses that reflect the characteristics of the Private Company we're attempting to Value.</u> Size, Sector, Profitability, and Growth Rate are crucial variables. You could also look at the amount of Debt and Cash flow in these firms. You can use it to track the stock market's performance against your expectations. Keep an eye on trends in the Business World, and find out how investors value current market situations.

2. **EBITDA Multiples:** EBITDA multiple is one of the most popular metrics Investors use to Evaluate a Company's Value. The Price to Earnings ratio, Sales to Book Value, Price to Sales, and Free Cash flow are examples of such measures. Calculating a company multiple is now straightforward, thanks to the Market Capitalization-to-Cash Conversion factor. The essence of the result is that we can compute and compare pre-tax multiples for different periods and firm and adjusted P/E ratios.

<u>The Company's Market Capitalization = [Price per Share] * [Total Number of Shares Outstanding].</u> So, you calculate an (Enterprise Multiple and divide it by EBITDA) to get the Company multiple. I've simplified it for you since it's a touch more complex.

3. **Comparable Transactions:** With Comparable Transactions, we're looking at Mergers and Acquisitions, Sector Activity, and identifying Comparable firms that have been acquired. The transaction data is then utilized to obtain benchmark valuations by comparing them to prior transactions. The disadvantage of this technique is that not all transactions provide Price and Valuation information.

49. What is EBITDA?

Let's figure out what EBITDA is all about. EBITDA is an acronym for Earnings before Interest, Tax, Depreciation, and Amortization. EBITDA is a popular proxy number widely used among Venture Capitalists and Private Equity firms. *It would be best if you fully grasped EBITDA, its use, and how we calculate it.*

EBITDA allows Financiers and Entrepreneurs to compare Profitability across Firms regardless of their Balance Sheet Structure or Financing Status. Interest, Tax, Depreciation, and Amortization are taken out when Calculating EBITDA. EBITDA eliminates the influence of Financing on some of the Critical Deal Structuring and Accounting Decisions for a PE transaction. EBITDA primarily indicates a Company's capacity to "Pay-Off" Debt. It's important for both Public and Private Equity firms. It's primarily utilized in Valuation ratios. EBITDA is critical for PE firms as their Deal Structures tend to be "Leveraged." EBITDA is one of the Critical factors that PE Firms consider while assessing a firm's Value; however, EBITDA is rarely used in isolation.

EBITDA is a Profitability Indicator. You may be led to believe that if you're making money, it'll automatically translate into more profits. But that's not the case. You must keep in mind that "Profit" and "Cash" are two separate concepts. Let's use a basic example to demonstrate how this works.

Let's assume a Firm generates $200 Million in Annual Revenue. As a result, it incurs an expenditure of $80 Million in Product Cost. Then there are $40 Million in Operating Costs. After Depreciation and Amortization costs of $20 Million, the Company's Operating Profit is $60 Million. Its Interest payments are $10 Million, and its Earnings before Tax are therefore $50 Million. With a 20% Tax Rate, its Net Income is $40 Million.

Now, we must retrace our steps to calculate EBITDA. The EBITDA is $80 Million. We add (Net Income [$40M] + Depreciation and amortization [$20M] + Interest Payment [$10M] + Taxes [$10M]). This clarifies EBITDA, its importance, and how to calculate it. It's a fundamental concept and an important number within the domain of Private Equity.

Section 11: Risks and Returns in Private Equity Investing

50. How to Assess Risk in Private Equity Investments

Let's take a moment to discuss the risks associated with Private Equity Investments from the perspective of the Limited Partner as an Investor. Limited Partners include high-net-worth individuals who add Private Equity to their portfolios to increase returns. Family offices are another example, where they're responsible for a family's assets.

Private Equity rather than Venture Capital is more relevant because Private Equity investments are generally in bigger, more mature firms with growth plans rather than much earlier stage, less established, higher-risk businesses. Venture Capital investments are usually more risky than Private Equity investments. Private Equity is a more established investment profile. Therefore, the returns are lower, but so is the risk.

So far, we've discussed how Private Equity investments use "Leverage" to increase the returns to Equity investors. They also attempt to manage their assets to boost yields actively. These traders aim to buy low and sell higher, making money from arbitrage. The beta aspect also contributes to growth during ownership, active Management, alpha factor, and external market conditions. There are restrictions to entry with Private Equity, especially regarding minimal investment. You can now get into a Venture Capital fund for as little as $500. Platforms such as Netcapital.com allow Startup Founders to Crowd-source fundraising. You get to "Play VC." It's a cool flex. I wouldn't expect anything from a Netcapital. Com-listed Startup, in any case. (*Private Equity Finance Made Easy is not associated with Netcapital.com or any of the sites mentioned within this book. Also, this is Not Financial Advice. Information is to be used for Educational Purposes Only).*

The most typical ranges for a PE Investment are between $5 Million and $25 Million. Institutional investors invest much money into this asset class, which may result in big returns and significant losses. Private individuals require a great deal of assets to participate in this market. The typical fund duration is ten years, and investors have little liquidity. And while they may get information on the performance of investee firms, they've essentially ceded control. They've handed over Management to the Private Equity firm and its team of experts, allowing them to handle it. They can also try to sell their interests in a subsequent transaction, which is frequently only feasible at a loss to the Net Asset Value.

Market risk is ever present. It's just one of those risks that come with any company. If it's a highly unanticipated risk such as a pandemic, you're in serious trouble if you own a restaurant chain. However, because enterprises are more established, better developed, and have a lower risk of default than earlier-stage firms, the risk is lower by default. In conclusion, Private Equity carries a higher risk than many other assets. The firms are highly indebted. They're striving to deliver a greater potential for profit while working to mitigate the leveraged risks that come with it. Whether you're investing in Private Equity or funds of funds, the general goal is to achieve a certain risk/return ratio as part of your investment spread. That gives you a sense of balance concerning the dangers of Private investments. It's unquestionably riskier than investing in pure quoted equities. But then you're banking on the abilities of the Private Equity house's investment team to build a portfolio that lowers a lot of corporate risks.

51. Equity in Leveraged Buyouts

Let's talk about the importance of Management Equity in Leveraged Buyouts.

Management Equity in Leverage Buyouts

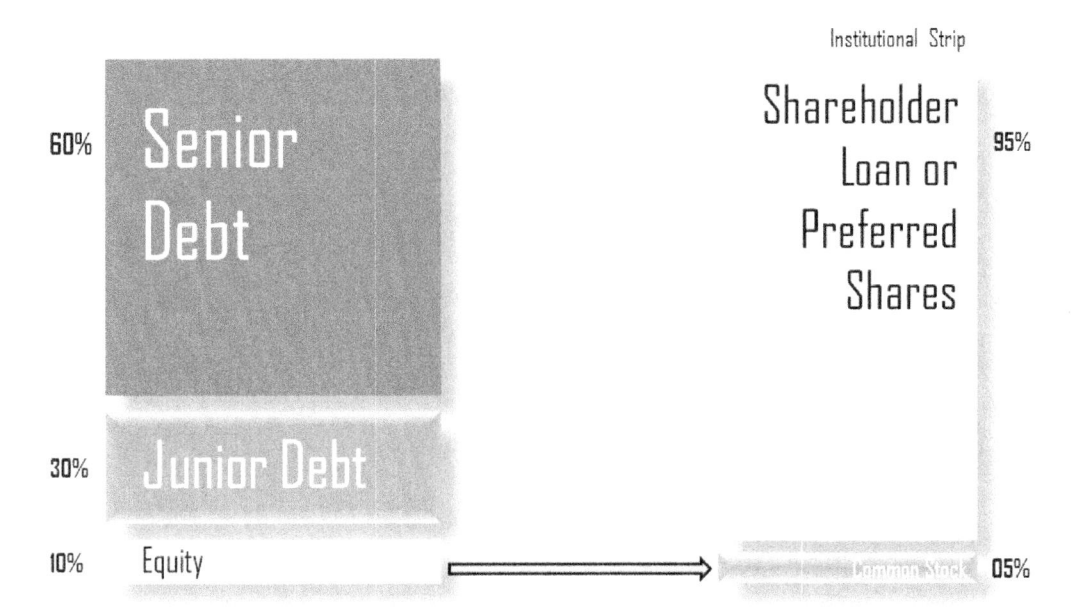

		Institutional Strip
60%	Senior Debt	Shareholder Loan or Preferred Shares — 95%
30%	Junior Debt	
10%	Equity ⟶	Common Stock — 05%

Ensuring Senior Management is rewarded well alongside Buyout firms and their Investors is critical. Management had a share in the Company before the Buyout, so ensuring they're incentivized is vital. They are expected to roll a significant portion of the new payment into the New Deal. Normally, more than 50% is rolled in. It is reasonable for the Management to want to cash out some of their Winnings, having previously owned the Equity and rolled it over.

In most cases, this is done to help individuals pay off their mortgage or save money for their kids' education. Private Equity firms still expect them to put a significant amount of their own money into the transaction if they wish to benefit from their expertise in the Future. Private Equity firms typically provide loans or set up stock option plans to enable the Management to have their Skin in the game.

Senior Management Share Options are known as "Sweat Equity," and they're called sweat equity because the Management is expected to "Sweat" it out and deliver growth KPIs (Key Performance Indicators). They're quite delightful. The terms are incredibly advantageous, and they're arranged to guarantee many returns above those received by Institutional Equity investors. But, as long as they have a large capital gain, that will be significant. They may still make millions if they put in tens of thousands of Dollars.

In contrast, Private Equity investors aim to double or triple their money. This might result in a 20 or 30-fold return. It's the sort of returns that the Management can expect to receive. Sweat equity also lowers costs because the options' exact price reflects the common stock's incredibly low Value at the time of the transaction. When you add the stock market and other assets, it's important to note that these option plans only pay out when the Company's Equity performs well. So it's a win-win situation: if the transaction succeeds, they do well; if the deal fails, they don't. They may only get their investment back or lose it. The overall objective of these alternatives is to align the interests of the Management and the General Partners.

However, as you can see from the structure, the General Partner usually gets excellent downside protection.

Management Equity in Leverage Buyouts

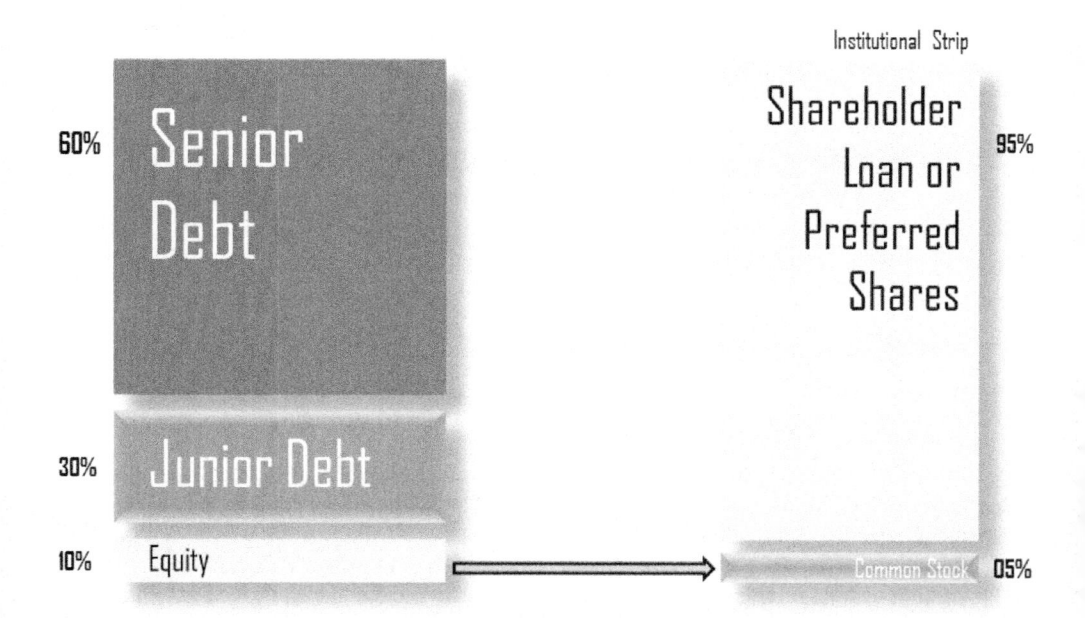

		Institutional Strip	
60%	Senior Debt	Shareholder Loan or Preferred Shares	95%
30%	Junior Debt		
10%	Equity	Common Stock	05%

Senior Debt is typically 60%. The Institutional strip is called the junior Debt or a Mezzanine component of 30% and the Equity Component. This is usually done so that 95% is Shareholder loans or Preference shares, with only 5% of Common Stock. As a result, the Straight ratio immediately increases to 20:1.

The fundamental point is that if you are a holder of an institutional strip, your base rate of return is safe, and virtually all of your money is protected (Up to 95% in most cases). With that shareholder loan or preference share, you receive a coupon, which must be repaid before funds are sent to the general stock. If Management rolled over or bought stock, they would receive a proportionate share of the common strip rather than simply common stock. They would be expected to put money in. If they don't have the cash, many individuals turn to their yearly salary as part of their new investment. We've already seen that some of it might be offered in loans. The institutional strip, composed of a mix of preferred shares and common stock, usually has an 8 to 12% coupon. This is intended to safeguard the General Partner and anyone participating in the Institutional strip. Once all coupons have been paid and the shareholder loans have been repaid, the remaining funds are available for common stockholders. But you can see that the common stock's Value is only one-tenth of the firm's Equity. If the sweat equity has the option to purchase common stock at that strike price, then the entire cost will be meager. The typical stock arrangement is usually set up so that most of it goes back to the General Partner, with around 80 percent returning to the General Partner. Around 20 percent are going to Management via their funds or Sweat equity, which we'll look at shortly.

The Sweat Equity becomes Common Stock, and each successful trade provides a 1:20 Leveraged Return. Here's the breakdown: You've got the Major Debt, the Minor Debt, the Shareholder Loan, and then this Tiny Little Bar at the bottom. And that's where all of your return goes. Sweat Equity amounts range from 10 to 20 percent of the Company's Stock. They're frequently defined as hurdle rates in the sweat equity agreements, which indicates that they won't stop until their goal return rate is achieved. The foundations for these things are in place. The IRR range is typically 20 to 30 percent or (2-3X) the Invested Capital. As a result, the deal must succeed before the Sweat Equity goes into effect.

The Sweat Equity generally spreads only to the C-Suite of an organization. The CEO might receive 4%, while the Chairman may receive 1%. The CFO gets 1%. The total C-Suite accounts for approximately 8% of the overall cost. Certain crucial people may share up to 2% for other executives and keep an unallocated portion of 14%.

The figures tend to change. The figures mentioned are for illustrative purposes only. There are Vesting restrictions linked to the Sweat Equity. <u>If the Management leaves before a specific date, they generally lose their Sweat Equity.</u> Labor conditions might be either beneficial or detrimental to the Management. It refers to the fact that if they leave and are considered a good leaver, they still retain their sweat equity, such as sickness or death during retirement. There is nothing perfect about most of those situations. However, the idea is that if employees quit the Company, they will not be able to take their ownership with them. Typically, Sweat Equity is associated with an "Exit" event.

As mentioned above, a separate stock option plan may exist for less senior workers. Still, its returns are nowhere near as generous as the sweat equity. Keeping the sweat equity and option pool unallocated is typical to allow for a fresh slate of hires and promotions. So that's a fast overview of Leveraged Buyout Management Equity. <u>The significance of this is to realize that even though Management is expected to have Skin in the game, their real returns come from the Sweat Equity. Sweat Equity is the driving force behind Incentive Compensation in any Agreement.</u>

Section 12: What Are the Exit Options When It Comes to Private Equity Transactions?

52. What is the Motivation for Taking on an LBO?

Let's have a look at what motivates a Leveraged Buyout. If you know why someone entered, you'll be better equipped to predict what they'll do to leave. LBOs can generally be divided into Four Categories.

So, when a company is taken Public by a Private-Equity firm, it is called "Repackaging." It could also happen when a firm is bought from existing shareholders and sold off shortly after. The idea is that the firm is kept for a few years, some restructuring may occur, and it's re-launched to the market several years later with a greater height to magnify valuations. Now, this has occurred a lot in the retail sector in the United Kingdom, where firms have been purchased and restructured by Retail groups. They were heavily indebted on the back of their property portfolios. So money was extracted from them and sold back to Public companies. Private Equity firms were able to extract an Exit through that process.

Much stuff has changed nowadays. If you can execute it in today's markets, it is a more intelligent business strategy. When a corporation breaks up, it resembles a typical business divorce. It happens to Public firms, frequently Multi-Billion Dollar Corporations, when the belief is that Sections are worth more than the Whole. So, the firm is broken up. There's a Multi-Step Exit to sell components of the Company for as much money as possible. As part of the deal, there are redundancies and reorganization. However, fragments of the broken-up firm could develop into Independent Enterprises in the Future.

Now, the Portfolio Scenario is simply a "Buy and Build." A Platform firm is bought, and additional rivals are added to it. Finally, the Entity is sold through a Trade Transaction to another far Bigger Competitor, or via an IPO. The "Rescue Scenario" has a negative side in mind. A struggling or failing firm is purchased at a bargain through a Leveraged transaction, often led by Management.

Let's consider why LBOs have occurred in the past.
- What is the purpose behind executing such complicated transactions other than creating Wealth?
- What is the goal of getting the contract done from a strategic standpoint?
- Another way to look at this is to consider where the Value is being transferred.
- Who is going to benefit from the deal? Because, you know, there will be a wealth transfer.

Financial engineering allows common stockholders to make high returns from successful transactions in an LBO. When a firm is taken Private, Reorganized, and Sold later, the Company may not change much. However, the previous stockholders effectively transfer any potential gain in the business to the Buyout Investors. As a result, the first to suffer are Public Bondholders, who no longer have access to company cash flows. When you look at the structure of the Buyout, you discover that the Debt providers who provide a significant portion of the Financing are receiving a significantly lower return because they have security and seniority in the Debt structure. Essentially, they're trading risk for safety by accepting a lower profit in exchange for greater protection. So, there's undoubtedly a net transfer of money.

The Management of the firm and its owners are incentivized to take various Growth-oriented initiatives as opposed to when it was previously held. Other benefits include the transfer of stock from the Government to Private Investment Common Stockholders. Because Interest payments are not tax-deductible, this is why the tax shield benefits of interest payments are lost. This lowers taxes and allows you to shelter your interest from taxation by amortizing Debt and making interest payments. Instead of paying taxes to the government on earnings, you may utilize them to repay the Debt. As a result, there's a wealth transfer from the government.

As you can see, one of the Primary motivations behind taking on an LBO is the process of "Wealth-transfer." Also, major "wealth-transfer" events occur around "Exit" opportunities. The next chapter will examine the LBO Exit options in more detail.

53. LBO Exit Options

Let's look at the possible Exit strategies for a Leveraged Buyout. When getting involved with Private Equity transactions, one of the first things you learn is that the Exit is considered carefully before initiating the Deal. It's one of the most important factors they consider when deciding whether or not to do a deal. It may appear odd that they would put so much effort into determining how they'll get out of a deal before they begin. As you go through this chapter, the PE firms' high intent focus on the "Exit" plan will start to make sense.

For starters, the investment return is dependent on the Exit plan. This is more than just a strategy for selling high and buying low. PE firms have to consider their Exit strategy and how they'll "Grow" the Value needed to achieve it before deciding to get in. They must also consider how the Exit will be appropriately carried out. The Exit is continuously reviewed throughout the portfolio lifecycle as the arrangement moves forward. If you're searching for M&A transactions, you must recognize that every Private Equity firm is always up for Sale.

An Exit can be accomplished through a "Trade Sale" to a Strategic Buyer, Financial Investor, IPO, or Liquidation. These "Exit" routes are characterized by the fact that the General Partners, Limited Partners, and Common Stockholders of the PE-controlled Firm have relinquished control.

PE funds can also obtain an Interim Rate of Return from their investments through Dividend payments and Recapitalizations. When a company performs exceptionally well, Debt is loaded into the business, and the PE firm pays itself a significant dividend from the Company's Cash reserves.

Another key element in Exits is Timing, especially in determining market conditions. Companies that sold out in 1998 and 1999 made enormous profits during the "Dot-com" Bubble. However, if they had sold themselves two or three years later, they would have made a fraction of those profits.

We'll look at IPOs and Trade Sales in upcoming Chapters of the book. I appreciate you sticking with me.

54. What is Recapitalization?

Let's briefly discuss "Recapitalizations" and explain what they entail for completeness. When Buyout negotiations are going exceptionally well, "Recaps" or "Recapitalizations" occur. The investors may expect a return on their money, which is frequently repaid in part or entirely. When a business's cash flow or earnings surpass estimations, this makes it possible to consider the possibility of "Debt-restructuring." This typically results in a large cash balance paid out as a regular dividend. As previously stated, this is not an exit but a chance to withdraw Cash from the transaction. Typically, you repay the pricey debts first. Then, suppose you still have Cash or in a few months or years when the money builds up. In that case, you may restructure and pay down debt, putting greater debts on the balance sheet, as the cash flow can handle it, and end up with a large sum of Cash in hand that you can extract through a dividend payment.

The chance to withdraw money from the transaction right now is excellent. They still have their ordinary stock. It does improve the Deal's IRR. However, the most significant benefit of a recap is reducing the risk of a particular transaction in the fund since you've already gotten most of your money out. That's what a recap is all about. Restructuring Debt and putting more Debt into the Company as long as the cash flows can support it is common.

Recaps don't happen very often, but when they do, they can be a significant advantage to Investors in the fund.

Section 13: Trade Sales with M&A

55. Company Sales in LBO Exits

Let's look at Company sales in the context of LBO. In the Private Equity World, a "Trade Sale" is the Sale of a "Portfolio Company" to another "Operating firm" in the same or similar industry Sector, such as a Competitor. Trade Sales are typical among firms with a "Strategic" need to do the transaction.

Strategic Investors are Firms who invest in a firm's shares intending to gain long-term Value. They have a long-term vision for your Company. Their Investment Strategy is not just financial but includes some financial elements. They generally attempt to Buy and maintain a company for the long term to gain market share and improve their Competitive advantage—strategic acquisitions result in improved financial performance, market entry, market share expansion, and product acquisitions.

My advice for you is to buy knowledge and insights by purchasing suppliers or distributors, synergies with existing goods, markets, and consumers, as well as intellectual property. These methods underlie the logic behind a high purchase price. Venture Capital firms prefer strategic trade buyers in Exit since they are seen as the most likely to pay the most money. In some circumstances, Investment banks are utilized to conduct auctions on behalf of the selling PE firm to organize the Sale.

Stock for Cash, Stock for Publicly traded stock, Stock for privately traded stock, and Asset sales are the methods in which the Value exchange occurs. In essence, what we're interested in is the Consideration. What exactly is being compensated for? Is it money? Is it a Public or Private Corporation? This is a huge difference. It's typically in the Acquisition agreement and Press release, but it significantly impacts Limited Partners. The most important thing to take away from this lesson is that following a Sale, Limited Partners would usually be rewarded with a Distribution from the fund relating to the transaction.

56. The Different Types of M&A Transaction Structures

Let's look at M&A transaction Structures in the light of an LBO Exit. You must comprehend what they are to determine whether a "Real" Exit exists. When a company sells a portfolio company in a trade sale to a strategic buyer, various alternative transaction agreements are accessible. These impact how the funds are dispersed to Limited Partners and whether or not the transaction is considered genuinely a liquidity event and Exit for the fund.

The First Structure is "**Stock for Cash**." This is the most basic and most frequent construction. In reality, the Private Equity firm selling the Portfolio Company's Stock receives Cash compensation. Following the agreement, most of the Buyer's money will likely be returned to its Limited Partners in proportion to their ownership interest in the fund. This is a straightforward cash transaction.

When a Private firm is sold, the fund may be given Publicly Traded Shares in the Company it sells to in exchange for its Consideration. You will also probably receive a combination of "Cash and Stock." The portfolio firm is incorporated as a subsidiary of the publicly traded strategic buyer. The fund may now sell the stock in the market, turning it into Cash, which he can then distribute to its Limited Partners. It's feasible, but it's unusual for the fund to send out the publicly traded stock directly to Limited Partners because they're primarily concerned with Cash. They don't want to deal with the hassle and administrative burden of keeping the stock they've traded.

However, there is a hitch to this: a problem that may make life more difficult. There exists a "Lockup." A "Lockup" is a form of precautionary investing. The fund's publicly traded shares are temporarily kept from being sold to maintain an orderly market in those stocks. This is usually done to ensure that the stock market remains stable. The typical practice is to have the investor distribute one-third of the Company's shares in phases, with the other two-thirds distributed later. This protects both sides by ensuring that any market sell-off does not happen all at once and destroys the share price of a publicly traded firm. The lockup can be for six to twelve months. The cash distribution occurs when the fund keeps the stock until they can arrange a sale, then the money is paid out.

In most cases, the investment bankers for a publicly traded company would, on behalf of the fund, manage the Sale of those shares in an organized manner to avoid affecting the market price. They'll also place goods with agreed purchasers rather than just putting them out to bid on the market openly. Lockups are one of the major reasons why Private Equity funds struggle to distribute profits. This issue cannot be overlooked, and it becomes a more challenging task. But you must first comprehend lockups and how they may affect the financier's capacity to disburse Cash.

A "Stock Swap" is not technically a "Liquidity" event or an "Exit" because the fund is exchanging one privately held stock for another. As a result, it's not really in a different position. Typically, the Buyer will keep the privately held stock in the business until it sells it for Cash or issues an IPO for its stock when a company purchases a portfolio company and then sells it for Cash. That's a Stock for privately held Stocks, which you must realize are essentially not worth the paper they're printed on. When the fund sells all of the portfolio company's assets for Cash, it is called asset sales. The Firm settles the portfolio company's creditors and distributes any remaining money.

In this structure, the purchasing firm, which is often a strategic buyer and could be an acquirer, does not assume any historic liabilities from the prior portfolio company. As a result, it's a simpler transaction to execute in comparison. However, it does present the Company with an issue: It must settle all outstanding creditors and wind up the Firm before distributing the funds to its Limited Partners. Mergers are the combination of two or more similar-sized firms.

In most cases, a New Co. is established to acquire shares in the merging businesses, which become subsidiaries of New Co. The proportion values of each Firm determine the number of shares exchanged. Suppose a split occurs 60-40 one way or 40-60 the other, depending on which way it goes. In that case, previous owners of the merging organizations will control proportionate shares of New Co.'s stock. Of course, this isn't a liquidity event until the large combined Company goes public or sells out.

When a PE firm announces a portfolio company, you can't assume it's an exit until you know more about the arrangement. **Specifically, if the PE fund receives Cash, it's an Exit.** It's a delayed exit in all likelihood if it were to be traded on a Public Stock Exchange. Furthermore, whether it is private or not has no bearing on if it is an actual exit. In the following chapters, we'll discuss each type of M&A transaction structure in the context of an LBO Exit.

57. Learning More about M&A Issues

Let's delve into some additional concerns that pertain to M&A transactions and LBO Exits. As we've seen previously, a transaction between a Portfolio Company and a Fund does not always result in an Exit for the latter. But there are a few more concerns to consider. The signing and announcing of a final agreement between the Portfolio Company and the Strategic Buyer is only authorized, but it's an intermediate step. It doesn't always guarantee that the transaction will be completed.

Closing conditions are a transaction agreement's provisions that must be met before the transaction can formally close. To give you an idea of what they are, Regulatory approvals and third-party consensus are a few to consider (this might be Property-related or Shareholders' Approval if there's a rights issue). The possible monopolies that may require antitrust clearance might delay closing a business acquisition. And it might be a few weeks before things are finalized. It might take as much as a month, but it can also take months, if not years, for the most significant and complicated transactions. It's also vital to recognize that a transaction isn't necessarily closed at the time it is announced. There's also the problem of Escrow. Some Consideration is kept in an Escrow account as a precaution against unanticipated liabilities emerging in the purchased Firm.

In other words, if I spend $100 on something, the lawyers keep $20. And suppose the purchasers discover things they didn't expect I hadn't revealed within a set time (six months or 12 months). In that case, they can reclaim $20 or part of the liabilities. So, you must look for any escrow arrangements in the transaction. If there are, then the chance that the Buyer will claw back any portion of the payment becomes more likely. Escrow can protect the Buyer because they may claim against items they discover in the Company that were not disclosed at the transaction time. For a Limited Partner, this might imply that anything from 5% to 20% of the sale consideration may be locked up for months or longer after the Closing.

The next thing to consider is that these are becoming increasingly rare. I've attempted negotiating announced, and it's nearly impossible. They're tough to negotiate and manage after closing the Deal. Buyers can negotiate lower rates than are available from the franchise and are likely to be more flexible on terms. They're usually wide open for gaming, so purchasers will run the Company over the earn-out period, distorting the business's economics but saving the buyer money. It refers to receiving a portion of the Consideration in advance. It is most often utilized to measure against agreed performance milestones. Suppose earn-outs are included in the package. In that case, Limited Partners will receive a delayed dividend. They must understand the owner's terms and realize that if the Company's performance doesn't meet the targets specified for the earn-out, later payments may not be made. Overall, the advertised price of a contract may differ from what is paid, and payments may be delayed for months or years without being made. These are issues that affect Limited Partners, and they're things we consider important. When you see an announcement for a Private Equity transaction, you should read it to discover the Deal's conditions and whether any concerns arise.

Section 14: IPOs - Initial Public Offerings

58. LBO Exits: Initial Public Offerings

Let's begin with Initial Public Offerings (IPO) as a method of Exit for Private Equity firms. When a Company sells shares to the Public, it's called "Going Public." An IPO is a Stock Exchange listing when a firm first sells shares to the Public by putting them on the Stock market. In the United States, a Lead Investment Bank or the Lead Underwriter files a registration statement with the Securities and Exchange Commission, then holds meetings with potential investors on a roadshow, then lists its shares on NASDAQ or the New York Stock Exchange, after which they are priced and sold to Investors.

I'll go through the IPO procedure in greater detail in the next chapter. However, in this chapter, I'd like to emphasize several issues and their ramifications for Private Equity firms and Limited Partners concerning the various requirements surrounding IPOs. When a firm goes Public or floats, it's typical for most investors, including the Private Equity group, to wait 180 days before selling any stock because of a "Lockup" period. Lockup aids in preventing significant share price decline by restricting selling investors from entering the market. So, the goal is to maintain a premium share price and keep it that way. So everything revolves around managing the successful IPO, keeping the stock price buoyant, maintaining a premium, allowing the Firm to settle down, and then only later allowing some of the existing shareholders to sell.

In the meantime, the Firm and the Limited Partners will suffer from delayed Exits. And this can result in a long wait for the PE fund to sell its stake in a corporation. An IPO, in general, isn't an instantaneous Exit for a Fund or a Limited Partner. The lockup expiration date is the date on which a lockup expires. As a result of this event, there may be many potential sellers of stock after that point, which may hurt the share price in the near term. When a lockup period ends, a Private Equity fund has three options. It can sell some or all of its shares on the public market. It can retain a portion or all its stock in the Firm and not sell it or distribute some of all the now freely tradable shares to the limited investors. A secondary offering can also be done if the shares are performing well. This may be done before the 180-day lockup expires. In a secondary offering, only existing shareholders sell stock. If a firm sells shares, it is not conducting a stock offering. A follow-on offering is one type of this; the two are quite distinct.

Insider Status: An officer or director of a business, or any shareholder who owns more than 10% of the voting stock directly or indirectly, is an inside person under US securities law. There's a huge risk that PE funds will own more than 10% of the business after an IPO or have a representative on the board and be deemed insiders. Insiders are assumed to have valuable, non-public information about the Firm, such as what's happening that hasn't been made public. This is completely natural because they're always talking to company directors. This is because, as insiders, they have certain restrictions imposed on them when and if they can sell their holdings. This has the potential to have an impact on LPs, too. Here are a few of my thoughts on Initial Public Offerings. They are an essential tool for LBOs to Exit their businesses. However, as you can see, they're quite complicated issues that don't automatically provide liquidity to the Fund or Limited Partners.

59. LBO Exits: IPO Process

Let's lay it out for the IPO process without being too technical. There are too many acronyms in this chapter, so bear with me. The IPO is a lengthy and complicated procedure. Let's begin by determining the major players in an IPO Process. Of course, there is the Firm itself. This Firm was the subject of a Buyout and is now a Private Equity fund-owned enterprise that wants to list it on the market. The following groups are the Investment banks, referred to as Underwriters. These individuals work for banking institutions (Investment banks). They are the executives in charge of the IPO process. They're a big deal, depending on the size of the IPO listing. There may be one lead investment bank and a team of other underwriters or many lead investment banks and other underwriters. It all depends on the scale of the IPO listing. The Securities and Exchange Commission, or SEC, is the next party to consider. Now you hear a lot about them. They are the Government Watchdogs who ensure that everything is done correctly. We also have the Attorneys (the people we adore), who do a lot of extremely hard and detailed work.

Next, the Team will develop this phase's main documentation and SEC filings. The accountants follow behind them and are in charge of all the financial work. They create and publish the Company's financial statements. The stock exchange, where shares are traded, is generally in the United States; it's similar to the New York Stock Exchange or NASDAQ, though it may be any European stock exchange. It should also be noted that before going public, a company's investors were known as market pre-IPO investors. So the stock in the IPO is bought by everyone, including the founder's buddies, angels, venture capitalists, and strategic investors, as well as our good friends at Private Equity funds and IPO investors - largely institutional investors. So it's an opportunity to cash out and make a killing. The new investors are no exception since they're looking for places to put their money.

Let's go through this one step at a time.
- The First Step is all about Preparation. This can take up to two years before the IPO takes place. If you want to run a successful IPO process, you must get your ducks in a row ahead of time. You must ensure you've found the proper management team, notably the CEO and CFO, with prior experience managing businesses in good standing. You'll need sound financial and management controls and procedures in place since you'll be expected to show that the Firm is running smoothly.

You'll almost certainly need an investor relations department, but particularly if you're a Startup and have no track record. You'll also need two or three years of historical, audited financial statements, which implies you'll want to get your auditors on board early and ensure they meet the expected standards.
- The Second Step is to choose an Investment Bank. Investment bankers now not only run the process, but they also underwrite it. So, if there isn't enough demand for the stock, they keep it, and the Firm still receives its money. That is the job of an underwriter. But you must pick the investment bank; these events are often known as beauty pageants. They'll invite several investment banks to come and pitch their services to them. Then, from the Group, a Lead Investment bank or more than one lead investment bank will be chosen. After that, those investment bankers and underwriters will choose the remaining underwriters participating in the transaction. Once they've gotten the investment banks on board, it's time to have the first meeting, when you set everything up and make everyone

aware of their roles. You must also resolve any legal and accounting concerns to guarantee that the SEC and regulatory filings go off without a hitch.
- This Third Step is known as the Kickoff meeting, followed by Drafting in the fourth Step.

We'll also need to start working on our registration statement, which is the S-1. The S-1 is a public document after it's filed. It does contain a wealth of information. And what happens is that an S-1 is created and submitted to the SEC. They offer input on it. It's much work, and the lawyer must go through several stages to ensure they've covered everything. It all starts when the lawyer receives a set of documents from the bankers. They must then go back and forth with them until they're satisfied. When you draft the listing particulars, you must fulfill all of the requirements in the listing document. You submit it to the stock market, and they respond with comments on what needs to be improved, and you continue fixing it until they sign it off. In the United States, smaller businesses may register confidentially under the Jumpstart Our Business Startups Act of 2012 to file with the SEC. Still, they are not required to do so.

- The Fifth stage is the SEC Review. The SEC will go through all of your documentation and share feedback to get them in their proper form before signing off on them. When finished, the registration statement may be formally submitted to the SEC. At this stage, the investment banks and Firms begin planning for the Roadshow.
- The Roadshow is the Next stage in the IPO process: The Firm and management go on tour for several weeks. They journey across the country, meeting up with investors and giving presentations to many potential investors about their Company. These investors generally require a management presentation and sometimes a video to convey the information to potential investors. These are usually institutional investors, although high-net-worth individuals can also be involved. Meanwhile, the underwriters of the investment bank are preparing another document for them called the "IPO summary."

This is the document that the IPO salesperson within the Investment banks will utilize to help sell the offering to Institutional investors through their channels. The decision on which exchange to utilize is a difficult one. The Firm could choose the New York Stock Exchange or NASDAQ in the US, the London Stock Exchange in the UK, or any of Europe's stock exchanges.

Of course, it may also be in Asia. A choice must be made regarding which stock exchange to list and if you're in the United States. The two most popular options are the New York Stock Exchange (NYSE) and NASDAQ. Then comes the roadshow, when the SEC filing has been approved and signed off by the investment bank, who have completed their due diligence and given their blessing to underwrite the Deal but haven't formally signed off on it.

The Roadshow continues to tour in order to introduce prospective IPO investors to its offering. This translates to two weeks of meetings around the United States, which is difficult. The Investment Banking Capital Markets Group begins its book-building effort at this stage in the process. This means they begin to keep track of the institutional investors' interest in the matter, how many shares they want to buy, and at what price. They begin by constructing the book to determine the demand, at what price, and from whom much stock is available. This is an essential stage in the process since they may make significant decisions that will have a huge impact on the success of the listing. The first is the price within the book. The company and investment banks will meet to establish a reasonable price for the issue, primarily based on demand and the number of shares offered in the IPO. Then, it's time to release the IPO. And, in reality, everything is completed the night before the market opens. The underwriters purchase the shares from the Company. Institutional investors buy them immediately after selling them to the underwriters. And then, on the next day, the bell tolls, and the stock begins trading on an exchange.

The IPO's early months are crucial for its Success. On the day of the offering, when a company first goes public, stock traders purchase shares at an artificially low price to market value (15% discount in most cases) to increase demand and drive up prices over time. Furthermore, this goal is to incentivize traders to do business with one another and stimulate prosperous trading by offering a first-day premium price that gets the whole IPO off on the right foot. The Firm went public after this. Let's move on to stabilization. I'm not going into the weeds, but investment banks must ensure that an IPO is successful and that the price does not dip below the offering price. They also undertake steps to stabilize the market and price for the Firm to start on the right foot as a listed company.

That's a brief overview of the IPO process. Of course, there is much more to it. It takes weeks and weeks, as well as months and months, of effort. It's much hard work, with late nights and meticulous drafting. You must double-check everything. The documentation never ceases to end. It's a complex process; however, there are the main steps to an IPO procedure. I hope you found it insightful.

60. Pros and Cons of an LBO Exiting an IPO

Let's look at some of the advantages and drawbacks of IPOs. However, an IPO is a company's most significant moment. It's not all rosy. You must also have a balanced outlook on the benefits and drawbacks of doing so. That's what I'd like to go over in this chapter.

Let's begin by considering the Benefits.

1. Access to Cash: Both in the IPO and the post-IPO period, when a firm has access to the stock market, it can raise capital, which means it may raise more money for follow-ons in secondary offerings in the future. This is a significant benefit to the Firm since it provides a source of liquidity.
2. Pre-IPO investors who invested in the Company before it went public can sell their shares. It offers a way out for Venture Capital and Private Equity firms, Strategic Investors, Founder's friends, and family members. If these are enforceable, the Venture Capital and Private Equity investors could be restricted by lockups and incentive restrictions.
3. A Public Company's Cash is a lot more flexible. It can purchase assets and use that paper to pay for Deals. You may now choose to go through a vendor or placing, which is the same as giving the paper straight to the Company's vendors. When you have decided on how much money you need to raise, you put that stock in the market, and then the Cash and Sale of those new shares are given to the people who sold the business. This allows the Company to start purchasing businesses and developing internally using paper and stock instead of cash reserves.
4. The Company is more reputable, which may benefit both Suppliers and Customers. They're also more likely to be in the news, particularly in the financial media, as a Public company.
5. Employee Stock Options can be beneficial; they might be immediately given to employees, which is excellent. The Company's attractiveness as an employer is further enhanced by the fact that it will be a Public firm, thanks to this whole IPO process, which adds significance and reputation. This also tends to have a significant impact on morale, which is why it's so important.

However, there are some limitations and disadvantages that we must consider and comprehend.

In the United States, the Securities Exchange Act of 1934 prohibits any person or organization owning more than 5% of a listed company's stock from making untrue statements in its annual reports. The next is reporting obligations. Public firms must provide quarterly financial and operational information to the Public. They are also required to disclose important events. Imagine if they make a large acquisition. It's a material event, and they'll have to report on it and give lots of information about it. The shift comes when the tech industry, in particular, faces increasing political pressure over privacy concerns and more public attention. There's been a significant increase in the number of people on social media networks, which puts them even more under the public eye and scrutiny than before — which has implications for how much management time is consumed dealing with this attention. There's a chance that management may shift to a more short-term-oriented technique if you consider that they must publish quarterly results, which greatly influences the stock price. Meanwhile, CEO compensation is tied to share price. They may be tempted to change their approach from long-term company development to short-term profit maximization.

There are additional expenses involved with being a public firm, including the IPO expenditures, the ongoing legal and accounting costs, and the expenditure of having your PR team and PR agents working. Confidential information is a more subjective but still important concern, and the filing process puts a substantial amount of company information into the public domain. This new information might expose an enormous number of previously unknown facts. It was unknown to people outside the Firm. This information covers companies, clients, goods, marketing plans, and everything else you can imagine about the Firm. Of course, this will be beneficial to rivals. They are opening their kimono if I use that phrase to provide their rivals more insight into the Firm than they had previously.

There's always the chance that activist investors will target the Firm if these investors generally focus on underperforming firms where they think there's an opportunity to significantly raise the share price by changing the strategy and undertaking extreme measures such as divestments. This might become a very time-consuming problem for management. It also costs the organization money. Activist Investors may be enticed to try and seize control of the Firm or force it to alter its approach to boost the share price, whether temporarily or permanently. And this can pose a significant management challenge. The short sellers are now aligned with the opposition, and they're people who believe a company's stock is overpriced and will fall. They sell goods they don't possess to either repurchase them later or have a contract to sell them at a lower price. They do this by selling their contracts on the exchange when the price drops, allowing them to close their position.

There is a problem with this because they tend to hurt the share price. Because they become so vocal about a firm's flaws once they've chosen to take it on, they may consume a significant amount of management time. The more information they can put out there, the more likely their predictions of a share price drop are to come true. The IPO may not be a success if the Company's share price does not perform well after the offering, which is known as a broken IPO, putting significant strain on management and their investment banking advisers to get the share price back up where they believe it should be, i.e., higher than the IPO price. That's a quick rundown of the benefits and drawbacks of being a Public Company during the IPO process, particularly from the perspective of the Firm and its leadership. However, you should know it is not an all-rainbows and sunshine affair. There are numerous difficulties connected with being a Public Company, some of which are good and others that aren't.

Section 15: Why Startups Fail?

61. Why Do Startups Fail?

What causes Startups to Fail? This is one of the most crucial and costly problems in business today. It is a well-known fact that 90 percent of Startups fail. This affair could be expensive for Investors, Venture Capitalists, and Angels. All the money contributed sometimes goes up in flames when a firm doesn't succeed and you decide to close it down. If you're a Startup founder, this is financially pricey and emotionally distressing. So it's a big deal and one that everyone should consider.

- How can you improve the chances in your favor, as they say in The Hunger Games, whatever your position?

Before improving our chances for Success, let's dive deeply into the major reasons for "Startup Failure." Understanding the reasons for Startup failure can help us avoid those traps and not become just another statistic in the graveyard of Startups.

While researching this subject, I found the CB Insights survey of Startup failure to be very insightful. I added one more factor to that list and organized these 21 problems into Categories. Based on my decade of entrepreneurial expertise, I will share my views on these issues.

Let's start by identifying the "Fundamental" issues. These can be identified before investing. These are at the heart of your business. If you're an "Investor" or a "Founder," you must be familiar with them. Next, we'll look at the "Post-Investment" external circumstances. These are things that can occur at any time. Frankly, they aren't always easy to identify based on due diligence, external forces beyond your Company's control. Then we look at "Operational difficulties," which are in the hands of the Startup, and they must be addressed with care. An outsider can discover "Management" problems and shortcomings long before they become evident by watching how the Company is run. Finally, I've got a few major "Financial Concerns" for you. These can be with the benefit of additional experience, glaringly obvious. Nevertheless, when you get to them, they appear as if they can be avoided.

Let's start by examining the "Eight Criteria" found in any Pre-Investment due diligence procedure in the following chapter. These are also critical for entrepreneurs, especially if they're new to the game. They provide a better picture of your product's weaknesses and flaws at its heart, so you'll have to work much harder to correct them.

This Section will get you thinking and help you avoid some of the most common blunders.

62. Why Do Startups Fail? Pre-Investment Strategic Issues

Let's look at what I've termed "Strategic Investment Concerns." These are fundamental problems at the core of every Startup endeavor. You could uncover them through the due diligence process. Investors will benefit greatly from these questions because they provide litmus tests that must be followed. These are issues that founders must examine very carefully.

The Seven most prominent of these issues are mentioned below:
- Lack of Market Need / No Market Need
- Wrong Team
- Unusable Product
- Bad Business Model
- Legal/Regulatory Challenges
- Lack of Passion
- No Investor Interest
- Section Challenges

Let's look at each one of these to get a better idea.

1. **No Market Need:** This is a serious warning sign. It's the most common reason for failure. And it should be something you pay close attention to. Said, does the Firm have clients? There are many fantastic technological concepts that no one will ever use. You may come up with infinite ideas, but will they benefit anybody? So, ask yourself: What issue are you trying to solve? How big of a problem is it for you? And does it have a large enough market and scale potential?

There wouldn't be a business without an answer to these foundational questions. Entrepreneurs frequently have a false sense of security regarding getting their consumers. You need to notice and understand whether the Firm is having difficulty developing customer interest because if it is, it might be a serious problem. What any Startup must seek to achieve is to address an important issue for others.

2. **Not the Right Team:** This is also essential. Is there a weak or missing link in the Team of founders presenting to you? And, if necessary, can you modify or fill those gaps?

<u>Is the current Team, as it stands, capable of developing and launching the product to market successfully? Or are they depending on freelancers or contract experts for some key talents?</u> Another concern is the Team Balance. Do the Team's personality and method of working together compensate for an out-of-control CEO? This can be as harmful as someone listening to and collaborating with their Founders. If the Founding team composition lacks inexperience, this can be built with external support systems. However, you must first determine that the Team comprises the Right Individuals. If you don't have the correct Team, this may be enough to convince you to walk away from the Deal. You may have a team in place that manages strategy. They can develop a product, but no one wants it. They're bad at following through. They have a product but can't consistently deliver it on time or of adequate quality, and their poor team-building skills are holding them back. The common saying is that 'A' players hire 'A' players, and 'B' players hire 'C' players because 'B' players don't want to work for 'B' players. So you can see the problem. Another notable statistic is that solo entrepreneurs take 3.6 times longer to outgrow the Startup phase than those with teams.

<u>So you'll need a Hipster hacker and a Hustler, a Designer, a Techie, and a Business guy on your Team.</u> And that's the foundation of a well-balanced group.

3. **Product Issues:** Bad user experience and unfriendly products are hallmarks of "Product-led" issues. People often try to construct what they believe they want rather than what they want. This results in products that are clunky and difficult to use. It's also not attractive. *Look at "Blockchain" based products, for example. They feel inherently complicated to use. I believe they were built by "Coders" for "Coders." And when they started getting mainstream attention, the users were left feeling a sour taste.*

   It's critical to ensure "Simplicity" of use. No iPhone ever came with a user manual. On the polar end, ask a "Tech-noob" to buy some Ethereum from Uniswap (*Sit back and watch them revel in misery*). Products should be entertaining, and they should definitely be what consumers want to buy. Focus groups and surveys don't count (Customer vote with their Credit cards). One method for ensuring thoroughness involves spending time with early adopters. Getting continuous ongoing feedback is an excellent place to start. The first release is never its final release. Products evolve over time, reflecting the product adopting itself to serve its core users better. Products typically built for core users are the ones that can branch out to serve a larger audience on account of their stickiness. "Instagram" was initially built with Photographers in mind. It has now evolved into an all-encompassing juggernaut of the Social Media World.

   If the Startup is Pre-sales, learn more about who the Leads are. Get an understanding of the Potential Customers the Startup is trying to serve. This will also help you get feedback from the Horse's mouth, the Customers / Early adopters of the Startups Products / Services.

4. **Excellent Concept / Product without a Business Model:** A product without a business model is a terrible business. Many of these may be found during the dot-com bubble. They will come if we build it, they promise. Well, I'm sorry to disappoint you, but promises aren't kept in that case.
   - How will the product make money?
   - The critical question is who will buy it and how much will it cost.
   - How can they convert a free service into a Paid one?
   - Can the product be expanded? It's a straightforward problem. Either the product makes money, or it doesn't. And if it cannot, you should not waste more time on it.
   - Is it truly Useful or Innovative? Is there a practical application for it, or is it simply a clever device or concept? Can you think of a method to grow your client base?

   The impact of this is that because the acquisition cost of a client must be far lower than the customer's lifetime value, any decision to acquire or retain customers should be based on metrics linked to net promoter score.
   - Can you make more money from your consumers than you spend to acquire them? In under a year, you should be able to recoup the cost of acquiring a customer.

   You may use These excellent metrics and tests to determine if a company's business model truly exists.

5. **Legal/Regulatory Challenges:** Legal difficulties can be costly. When conducting your investment due diligence, you should look for unresolved legal issues. One of the ways that competitors compete in this market is by responding to a disruptive challenger by filing lawsuits against them. When such challenges come from a major competitor with the resources to drag you through the courts as an investor, this should be a warning flag. These difficulties may emerge later on, and the ideal response may be to retreat and pivot rather than to fight.

6. **A Lack of Passion:** A Lack of Passion among Startup leaders can be disastrous. They must be passionate about their business and the area in which it operates. And, if they're only looking at how much money they'll make, you should move on. This becomes apparent after chatting with the management team. It's worth watching how they talk about the Company and how they think.
7. **No Finance or Investor Interest:** Before investing in your angel round, anticipate the Series-A round and how those investors will react to your Firm. Look at the most significant trend in the market and the sector.
- What is the state of the overall environment?
- How competitive is it?
- What comparable offers can you find?
- You may be already too late. The train has departed, and at least two or three well-funded businesses are doing what you're doing. It will be impossible to attract other investors if you can identify some likely major investors with deep pockets early on. Furthermore, they don't have any conflicts of interest, such as having invested in the domain previously. You could discover that your Company is suffering from a location problem. For example, you could have many investors in San Francisco but no London startups.
    - Suppose a major competitor has already completed a large amount of capital raising. In that case, it will have the financial and investing resources to win at all costs. If you're unsure, look at any company attempting to compete with Uber in the taxi sector or Airbnb in the flat rental industry. You'll discover that competing with a well-funded, large-scale player is very tough.
8. **Sector Challenges:** There's a lot of Sector prejudice, faddishness, and trends that may influence whether or not investors want to invest in the sector. You also have certain traits in specific industries. The difficulty is that if you don't understand the sector, you must be especially cautious about how you invest. Companies dealing with software may get so caught up in their technology that they lose sight of their clients. It's difficult for startups to gain traction, and they frequently find it tough to develop a workable business model. There is no simple route to establishing a viable company model in the mobile apps market. Can money be made via Mobile Apps today? It's much easier to create a business in the fashion sector. There may be cash concerns. You get a lot of highly creative individuals, but they might not always be as focused on their financial well-being as they should. Failure to receive funding or running out of money is a typical issue in the music business. There are several technical problems, as well as several legal difficulties, from the incumbent businesses that are attempting to preserve their turf in the industry.

So, <u>what sector experience do you have, and which sectors will you focus on to ensure you understand the Firm you're investing in?</u> That's all there is to it. I won't go into detail about each of them because they're self-explanatory. Still, there are a few more items to consider before investing based on my previous experiences. In the following chapter, we'll look at some "External Concerns" that may only surface after a purchase. You'll have to dig deeper into these issues, especially if you're an Investor making a Venture investment or a Startup Founder and need to figure out why it's suddenly failing.

63. Why Do Startups Fail? External Problems (Post-Investment Issues)

So far, we've discussed "Eight Concerns" that might arise during Due diligence before an Investment is made. Now, we will look at "External Concerns" that may emerge after an Investment has been made.

1. **Get Outcompeted:** There's much Competition in the Market, and you need to be aware of what your competitors are up to. Don't think the First-Mover advantage is enough to carry you through. More often than not, <u>if you have a fantastic product or service in an enticing market, you'll attract a slew of imitators who will compete with you.</u> You must maintain constant vigilance. You've made your wager as an Angel Investor or Venture Capitalist. However, This does not imply that you cease monitoring the other players at the casino table.

It's conceivable that the technology your product needs to launch isn't yet available. Do you know whether you're dependent on other markets' success for your company's own? Take a case of VR headsets. If the Market isn't mature enough or the adoption rates of VR aren't primed yet, you might be entering the market too soon. It could also happen that the Market is moving too fast for you to evolve. For example, when ChatGPT came out, it completely obliterated every AI Writing tool on the market that was built using OpenAI APIs or wrapper Startups that used OpenAI models instead of building their own.

Ignoring user feedback is a big mistake.

- Can the Startup team Identify issues as they are seeing them?
- Do they have tunnel vision in creating the product to the point that they overlook apparent flaws?
- Are they spending enough time interacting with clients? This can be done as an Angel Investor or a Venture Capitalist. You could get specific consumer feedback on the product you're currently using.

2. **Premature Expansion:** The more a Firm expands, the farther it gets from Profitability. As a firm Scales ahead of Sales and Revenue, the Cost base goes up. This typically results in all accessible cash being spent on even more expansion. You've got Scaling, Recruiting, and Growth to deal with. All of these become challenging at times. And 70% of Startups Scale prematurely. Furthermore, this can cause serious issues in their growth curve further down the road.

In essence, the goal of a Startup is never to be a Startup. It's always about progressing past that point. You can see when Startups are potentially unprepared by looking at key metrics and critical red flags. When a Startup has no idea how long its customers will be loyal, it faces several difficulties. This is most likely due to the fact that the clients haven't been around for long enough. It also indicates a lack of maturity if your company doesn't acquire consumers repeatedly. You've got a methodical, low-cost way to get customers started. Still, you're probably not ready to scale it because you have no idea how to grow and leverage your user base.

If you spend more time repairing things in the business than developing it, keep working on it until it's ready.

- Have you found your Problem-Solution fit yet? You could be selling to people who don't know you or what you're selling. And you might not have gotten to a place where lower cost of customer acquisition and increased revenue can help you achieve profits. If you're still having trouble with any of these, it's probably not the time to Start Scaling. It's obvious to make errors when attempting to expand across the Globe. The location must be in sync with the growth.
- Another thing to consider is that the money goes where you're growing the most. So if your Company's based in New York, there's no assurance it'll take off in San Francisco or London. Another indication of a successful business is whether it can expand beyond its borders. Suppose you've seen the Facebook movie The Social Network. In that case, you'll remember that they began at one university before trying to gain traction in additional schools. That was a geographic indicator of scalability, an absolute classic case. Another reason for the problem could be that you're employing remote workers. These can be a real pain regarding collaboration, communication, and cooperation. The issue of geography may be due to where your staff is situated and how they collaborate. So please don't be ignorant of it.

We'll look at "Internal Operational Issues in the next chapter. We've looked at some External difficulties that might impact the Company, and now we're going to look at some Internal Problems. Many different factors are involved in determining a Business's success, including what was promised to Customers, Competition, and Management decisions. This book will help you understand how businesses succeed or fail to get where they want.

64. Why Do Startups Fail? (Internal Operational Problems)

This is a list of the most common mistakes Startup businesses make in the United States. These range from anything to do with "Cost and pricing," "Ineffective Marketing," "Ignoring Consumers," and "Lack of Pivoting."

1. **Cash flow & Pricing:** The goal of any Startup is to ensure that they charge enough to cover their costs while being competitive enough to grow into a larger business. The other side of the equation is "Cost Management," which ensures that Profits can be sustained. It's critical for both "Founders" and "Investors" to spend time learning and evaluating the Fore-cast Projections. It's essential to have a more profound understanding of "Fore-casts," where you can explain precisely how much money will come from where and what they'll sell.

- Will they sell it outright, or will they sell it through a Dealership?
- How much are they hoping to receive in return?
- When are they going to sell it?
- Who are the consumers? And what does this imply in terms of getting started?
- Is the Product or Service being proposed in a specific quantity and quality feasible for them to do so on time?

The significant challenges are, first and foremost, the "Product & Service Pricing Assumptions." The litmus test for this is whether or not the original assumptions are being fulfilled early on. Early failures to achieve even modest amounts of sales might be a red flag that something much more severe is on its way. Another approach to view it is to consider if there's a better way to charge for the product or service, making it simpler for clients to comprehend while still providing enough money in the business.

When you consider specific internet models, try to learn why they're "Subscription-based" or "One-time" Sales. There is a lot one could discuss about how to price a product or service; at the very least, consider whether there is a different option.

2. **Ineffective Marketing:** Unsurprisingly, ineffective marketing is widespread within the Startup ecosystem. Many Founders and entrepreneurs are a group of really nice but geeky guys who understand how to design and develop a product. They don't know how to market it. You should make sure they understand their Market. They know how to gain the attention of their clients. They know how to turn their customers into sales and then teach them how to pass the word about the product or service to grow. If you're a VC or Angel Investor and your team consists of only coders or geeks who adore developing the product but don't know how to sell it, you have a problem. You can help them address this vulnerability by recruiting a CMO. One of the problems that will become more apparent is that the firm does not develop enough traction fast enough.

- Is it possible that the founders may have overlooked customers, who are so enthralled with growing the company that they haven't spoken to their consumers in a long time?
- Is there a customer feedback mechanism in place?
- Is the product's roadmap keeping up with consumer demands?
- Do they address the desire to build a truly unique product or the team's interest in creating something unusual?

- Is tunnel vision an issue? You must urge the team to stay in touch with consumers and provide them feedback regularly, ensuring that the company's founders are doing so.
3. **Failure to Pivot:** Pivoting is, without a doubt, a difficult and hazardous position. In many cases, it's a make-or-break situation since the company's initial attempt has failed, and you must rotate 180 degrees, 190 degrees, or 90 degrees to try to salvage the trouble. So you're already at a critical point, and if you don't pivot away from a bad product, a poor hire, or an ill-advised decision soon enough, you'll find yourself in serious trouble. If you wait too long, you'll likely run out of money before the pivot can succeed. If your market changes, you must be prepared to adapt. Pivoting is a good thing when it comes to coping with unexpected developments. If the need arises, you must act swiftly and firmly.

These are some of the "Internal Operational Concerns." These are problems that can be addressed and avoided rather than being 100% effective all the time. You didn't fall off a cliff, at least, without seeing them coming. In the following chapter, we'll examine problems particular to "Startup Management."

65. Why Do Startups Fail? What Are the Most Common Key Management Issues?

Let's take a look now at some "Key Management Issues." In the previous chapter, we examined "Operational Problems," which might lead to failure. We'll look at "Management-related concerns" such as "Lack of focus," "Disharmony," "Lack of Use of the Network," and "Burnout" in this chapter.

You can also observe how these factors are all highly personal to the Founding Group, starting with:

1. **Lack of Focus:** As a Company grows, the initial team faces a slew of new difficulties, including dealing with Investors, Employees, and Clients, as well as answering to the Board of Directors. This may weaken their attention or, in the worst case, negatively influence the product and customer experience. The problem is that the Founders are enthusiastic about developing their product. Still, they're not particularly enthused about running a business or focusing on a particular domain in their field. As an investor, you have a duty and an opportunity to intervene as a mentor and guide in order to prevent this from becoming a problem.

   You'll need to bring in a professional business manager, leaving the original team to focus on developing the goods and services. When individuals begin to lose attention, you should bring them back to focus. With this type of management, you can focus on customers and the product rather than having endless coffee conversations with individuals who want to pick your brain. You don't need to use "Networking" as an excuse not to address problems any longer. You may also abandon the practice of seeking out "Advisors." You may no longer enter into partnerships that don't appear to provide a lot of financial gains. In the short term, you may stop a substantial amount of public relations since it's a complete waste of time without a product or service. You can hold back on releasing much information on social media until you've correctly established your service. And, you may stop going to conferences, regardless of how much fun they are. These are some of the first warning signals. All you want to do is pull them back so they can focus on the product and the consumer.

2. **Disharmony**: Disharmony has a way of cropping up within a Business arrangement. It might exist within the team and between the Team and Investors. This is a challenging situation since the team may not function effectively, investors may enter the scene, and the team might become irritated with their involvement in the company. You can't afford to miss out on a good deal because of a so-called "disagreement" that doesn't affect your job prospects. If you find yourself in this situation, you must immediately resolve it by re-strategizing the team or avoiding investing when there is an investor quarrel. This might signal the end of the line for your business. It may mean curtains if it's a "Series Investor" pursuing the original round after it closes. If the investor decides to withdraw and leave the firm without any financing, it will be forced to shut down. (*Trivia: OpenAI almost collapsed when Sam Altman refused to let Elon Musk run the Show, and Elon withdrew his investment.*) Be wary of potential warning signals, and do your best to correct issues before they become critical.

3. **Didn't use Network:** If you're an ABC angel investor, you may actively intervene to prevent this since you'll have a strong network of people you can utilize to assist your investing enterprises. Now, Startup teams can't accomplish everything alone. Consider the makeup of any advisory board and consider whether there are any limits or anything

you can do to improve it. Of course, one of the first things that comes to mind is whether or not there is an advisory board. Consider how your network and the networks of those involved in the startup's success could be put to good use. This is something you may contribute a constructive external viewpoint to.

4. **Burnout:** Because overwork is a way of life (*Millennials, say "Hey"*), "Burnout" is a severe problem. The work-life balance is a disadvantage in these companies' Startup cultures. I appreciate their work ethic, but it can become excessive at times. A balanced team that can share the responsibility is critical, and delegated authority is non-negotiable. You must ensure that this happens. Angel Investors or Venture Capitalists must be looking for indications of this occurring and prepared to intervene before things get out of control.

So these are some major management concerns you should be aware of and alert to as an external Investor since you can act to solve them. Even as a Founder, if you witness it happening around you, you have the power to address the problems before they become fatal. The following chapter will focus on the last category of critical problems, encompassing all aspects of "Financing."

66. Why Do Startups Fail? Finance Problems

This chapter will examine a few pressing "Financial" concerns. We previously looked at management-related problems that may be deadly. We'll explore the fourth category, finance, and two critical issues in depth.

The first one is self-explanatory:
1. Running Out of Money
2. Pivot Gone Wrong

So the firm ran out of money. Yes, this does happen more often than you would expect. The question is how the firm should spend its money. The issue is that you've just raised a significant sum of money. You have a certain amount of runway, which is the number of months left in your burn rate before you run out of cash and need to prepare for the next funding round. This should be implemented with clear milestones in place. It's not enough to believe we have a lot of money in the bank and can now spend it on anything we want. A company running out of cash is typically due to a lack of excellent financial management and controls. A firm goes bankrupt because it failed to manage its existing resources adequately, leaving insufficient time to raise the next round of capital.

When you're done raising funds for the previous round, you've got to work on raising money for the next. And it's not difficult – many firms have already started preparing their second funding round after they've completed the first one. You can do this as soon as you close your current fundraising effort. I'd go as far as to say that the CFO should know precisely how much cash he has in the bank every night at the close of play, down to the penny. It demands careful adherence to procedure. It's also the obligation of the Company's founding team and management, notably the CEO and CFO, to act quickly to ensure that the financing takes place in a timely manner. One method to look at this is to set clear objectives. And, as the company's value rises, so does the risk of losing it entirely.

Let's review some of the Milestones Founders could follow:
First and foremost, you can reduce the dangers of Bankruptcy by "_Recruiting people who know what they're doing._" You could also work around any technological hurdles while developing the product by creating a "Prototype" and getting it into your first customers' hands quickly. You can conduct a successful beta test, get consumer validation, and start selling. These factors and the others listed above confirm and encourage investors to be more comfortable with the firm. Correct your Product-Market fit with a more updated feature set to close gaps in the original release. You can show your business model to consumers and start scaling, and you can ensure that your customers have a low cost of acquisition. You may also raise more cash at a higher valuation to speed up growth or expansion if you've shown that you can scale. Take the initiative and seize the land as soon as possible, or make sure you have enough working capital to expand. The failure to meet milestone expectations, of course, has a detrimental influence and might result in a value drop or the inability to raise cash at all. Remember, Cash is King for Startups, and Investors will notice if you're desperate and running out of money. They'll either walk away or offer you a derisory price that you'll be severely fleeced. As a result, you must take measures to ensure that your funding raise is completed on schedule and correctly.

2. **Pivot Gone Wrong:** The other problem is when the "Pivot" fails. This is another instance of running out of cash. It's a desperate attempt to keep a firm alive before it goes bankrupt. While the technology and vision are excellent, it's likely to fail if there isn't a compelling need or opportunity to scale. As an "Angel" or a "Venture Capitalist," keep your eyes and ears open to ensure your firm functions effectively. And if it isn't, and it's considering a pivot, you should ensure you get involved so the decision to change course can be made quickly. It's the correct decision. It's a good pivot. And it will result in successful company preservation as every pivot is essential to a firm. But all of that isn't very meaningful if you don't get the numbers right. And if you mess up, sooner or later, you'll most likely collapse. However, attempting to pivot before you're successful will result in the company running out of money and forcing you to shut down.

That is a list of pressing issues that lead to a Startup failure. Can you think of any more? Please write to me if you do Umran@onecallbusinesssolutions.com. Please appreciate how important cash management and financial management are to any firm. And if those elements of your company are inefficient, you're likely to fail. Suppose you're trying to figure out why a company or startup fails. In that case, one of the reasons is that it may have Overlooked Critical Warning Signs. You can prevent future problems before they become serious by recognizing these signals and acting on them early. I congratulate you on your accomplishments and hope your efforts pay off for you and your company. I wish all the best for you, as well as any other Rum enthusiast reading this book.

Section 16: Fund Performance of Private Equity Funds

67. How Do I Go About Evaluating Private Equity Fund Performance?

Let's look at how Private Equity funds perform in the Market. As you anticipate, I'd like to add some intelligent meaning to what we've learned thus far. This issue of evaluating fund performance is not simple. There's a lot of financial complexity involved. And when it comes to assessing performance, we need to speak about some of these issues rather than just relying on fundamental ratio analysis.

"The Vintage Year," the year of the fund's first investment, may be used to compare similar funds when assessing their performance. That's one of the reasons why it's so helpful. You should be aware of a problem between "Interim" and "Final" performance. This must be carefully considered while a fund still has investments since the returns may not yet be finalized. Early results may be deceptive owing to the fact that fund valuations have a tendency to be faulty throughout the life of a fund. They might achieve a spectacular return on one investment early on and mislead investors.

Furthermore, we may have valuations in the fund that are either high or low. As a result, you're all over the place until an established track record for selling numerous assets develops. This compels me to urge caution when evaluating any interim fund results.

You'll need to determine whether the returns that are being offered to you are "Gross" or "Net." This implies that Limited Partners evaluate Net results after deducting all Management fees and other costs. However, the Gross returns from a Partnership's portfolio investments are limited to the number of gains not offset by expenses and taxes. The General Partner subtracts the carried interest.

So, is a fund's IRR of 28% excellent or terrible? I'm asking you to consider this question because I want you to think about it, maybe even put the book down for a moment. The short answer is, "it depends." The basic response to the question is that you don't have enough knowledge to answer and should ask further questions.

The first question is,
- Whether the IRR is based on Gross or Net Returns? We've already gone over that subject.
- What is the fund's vintage year? Because the period may be flattered if the fund is less than two years old. The time you hold security and the price at which you buy or sell it has a major impact on IRR computations. The good news is that it considers the time value of money. If the return is straight, there'd be no question of multiple on the returns. However, if it were greater than one year, it would be preferable if it were over five years since the rate would be lower. You can earn a far higher IRR in one year than over five years. However, you must continue to drill down further.
    - You'll want to ask about a Fund's Growth Strategy. For example, Venture Development or Buyout Recovery? We don't know if a 28% IRR is a desirable Buyout or Secondary fund. You also don't know what the time frame is. Then, similar funds have done quite well with Comparable Approaches, using identical years and fund sizes in comparable sectors, regions, and countries. How difficult can it be to offer a simple answer when the factors are this complex? Is this an advantage or a disadvantage? So, what can we take away from all of this?

Multiples vary over the fund's lifespan, and IRRs can be boosted by brief periods. So you can't just accept everything you see at face value since the multiples might be flattering, or they may be understating the fund's performance. It all depends on how the "Exits" are handled and particularly which "Exits" are taken. <u>You must study the specifics of each "Exit" carefully.</u> You should be cautious about accepting returns on the fund since they are interim rather than definitive. It's too simple to assume that the fund's return is in 2 or 3 years. Values in the fund might not be accurate despite the obligation being on the fund to represent net asset values at fair market value. And this isn't a black mark against the funds. This is another example of how difficult it is to Value Private Firms, as seen throughout the book. This implies that the residual values, the funds quote, are mostly best estimates and must be treated as such. The higher the residual values in a fund because these can alter, the greater the potential for downside risk in that fund. You also need to consider it before investing.

Once funds have been raised after two or three years, they begin to invest, but the fundraising team doesn't rest for five years. It begins to raise the next fund, and it gets on. They will then present their most recent fund as part of their track record. And keep in mind that a ten-year fund with a two- to three-year track record has drawbacks. You must be critical of the data they're looking at. It's critical to take a closer look at the timeliness, exit, and accomplishments in such a short period of time. You must examine each transaction and the residual value in the existing fund, as indicated by the points I've made thus far in this part of the chapter. So, it's not straightforward, and it's an intriguing topic. I could write a book about fund performance that could stand independently. This chapter provides you with some perspective and insights into how you might measure funds. It is also to inform you about the complexity of the problem. My primary aim for you is not to accept everything at face value but to be prepared to ask further questions, dig deeper, and maintain a critical view.

68. What is the ROI of Private Equity Funds?

Let's get beneath the surface and determine how Private Equity fund profits are calculated. We must tie all the loose strings together to understand Private Equity fund returns. We've gone into a lot of this previously in the book. Still, I'd like to reemphasize it since there's so much information to cover, and it might be difficult. Private Equity firms aim to own a majority or controlling stake in private businesses. They use their skills to increase performance by making changes such as management modifications, strategic redirections, and product portfolio development and optimization. These corporations aim to maximize returns for their investors while maintaining Profitability.

We've already seen that they use **Arbitrage** (Buying low and Selling high). They use **Leverage** to boost returns to equity. They utilize **Alpha Growth**, which is direct growth resulting from management activity, and **Beta Growth** over time (growth attributable to the Market) to get these profits. They flee to various Exits, including IPOs, Trade Sales, Mergers and Acquisitions, and Secondary Transactions.

Let's take this a step further and consider the General Partners: Private Equity men who work inside a firm and get compensated through Management fees and Carried interest. Limited Partners are taxed lower than General Partners because they are not entitled to any portion of General Partners' return. Limited Partners earn an income from the 80% of returned funds left after accounting for the carried interest of the General Partners, Portfolio Company Earnings, and minus Management Fees. All of this is laid out and governed in the General Partners and Limited Partners partnership agreement.

Things become more challenging as Private Equity firms employ sophisticated investment structures to boost their profits. Furthermore, this accounting is influenced by the fund's jurisdiction and the accounting standards that apply there. Now, to emphasize this difference, I'm not going to get into too many accounting details because there are a lot of them. I'll mention one or two things, but you need to internalize that, and we'll move on to the more vital aspects of the discussion. The degree of influence impacts how much the fund manager can be influenced by what is happening in the Market. An example is the UK, where equity accounting is needed for important minorities, such as 20% to 50% representation on boards. However, under US GAAP, unless the partners have a written agreement allowing them to redeem their investments and select a time, that is treated as equity in the US.

In the United Kingdom, partner capital is considered debt with a limited duration. As a result, there are two distinct approaches to things. On entry and exit, the returns to funds are obvious: you know what the entrance prices are when a sale occurs or when an Exit is achieved, and there is a market valuation that may be measured in the following time period and taken into account all of the accounting restrictions. The valuation and profits must be comprehended to evaluate fund performance. This is more difficult than it appears, not just because they are privately owned businesses, but also because of their complicated financing structures and diverse ownership levels.

On the other hand, the accounting standards insist that funds be recorded at a reasonable value in their books. Does this help? No, because it isn't a precise definition and varies between accounting rules.

Generally Accepted Auditing Standards (GAAS) in the United States require Private Equity firms to follow a framework established by the CPA (American Institute of Certified Public Accountants). The United States needs a cash flow statement, an asset and liability statement, a planned investment schedule, a statement of operations, notes to the financial statements, and separate listings of any financial achievements. The United Kingdom requires a P&L (Profit and loss) statement, a balance sheet, a cash flow statement, and account notes. So, it's unique. As a result of this, the treatment of funds is challenging. It isn't easy to quantify a firm's "Worth" while a fund holds it before an "Exit" is reached. In the next chapter, we will look at how funds structure their finances and the relationship between the General Partner, Limited Partners, and subsequent impacts on fund returns. Before we look at some of the key ratios used to measure returns, I'll explain some of the crucial terms you need to know. This is a step-by-step development process. We've learned about the investment structure and strategy and the complexity of different accounting rules, fund structures, and corporate governance standards. Now it's time to look at the important terms and phrases that allow us to start defining terms and defining ratios, as well as their meanings. When we can apply the ratios, we can compute the returns. That's where it all starts. You will understand how these are calculated by walking you step by step through the framework.

69. Defining Private Equity Fund Returns: What Do They Mean?

Let's take the "The PE fund returns" debate and see if we can determine some important terms. We've seen that General Partners receive a Management fee (typically 2%), and have a "Carried interest" in fund returns. Two provisions influence the Preferred return and the Capital Clawback in the Partnership Agreement. Preferred return or Hurdle Rate is an important concept to grasp. The return to Limited Partners before the General Partner interest kicks in is known as the "Preferred return" or "Hurdle rate." And this is generally around the eight percent mark.

Investors with Limited Partnership stakes must generate at least an eight percent return on their investments before the General Partners can profit from their carried interest. The **Clawback** provision is the other side of the coin. Suppose losses erode overall fund performance later in the life of the fund. In that case, the fund may claw back a portion of the Limited Partners' profit. So, it prevents the Limited Partners from being overpaid and the General Partners from absorbing all the losses because the early portions of the fund were paid too much money. Even the committed capital and drawdown are important to grasp. When Limited Partners join up to their Limited Partnership agreement, they commit an investment amount to the fund. This is not paid out on the first of each month but rather due to fund investments made. **Drawdown** is the name given to this process. The first year the fund takes capital from investors is known as the **Vintage year**, which follows after the fund's start date. The cumulative amount of money invested in a company by an investor at a certain time is **Paid-in capital**.

The "**Invested Capital**" is the amount of money put into organizations. Some may be paid in the capital ready to be invested or on the verge of being invested. There's always a difference there, however. When assessing its investment performance, you must know the amount and timing of the fund's total distributions. This is everything that the fund pays out in stock and cash to its Limited Partners during a given period. So now we're talking about money that has gone in. Now we know what residual value is. The market value of the remaining equity that Limited Partners have in the fund is another key term. The funds also assess their investment firms' net asset values. So, with the net asset value of the companies in the fund, the Limited Partners can work out their percentage interest in those companies, and they can come to a residual value.

Suppose you compare the residual value of the fund's remaining assets with the original purchase price. In that case, you may evaluate the potential unrealized profit of those remaining assets. You can thus evaluate the project's initial costs. So you know what the firm would have cost when it was still in progress. It may be 100, the company's residual value, or the firm's net asset value is 150. In other words, the fund will be able to work out its proportionate share of that 100 and 150 less any distributions made in connection with the asset have been used to create a value for it. The residual value is determined by Limited Partners, generally quarterly. It is published by the fund quarterly to evaluate current performance. Hence, the residual value is an essential notion to grasp.

Now that you've learned what all these words mean, it's critical to grasp them because they are some of the factors used to assess Private Equity fund performance and returns. And that is why we have covered them in this chapter.

70. Return Ratios for Private Equity Funds

Let's look at some Private Equity return ratios, worldwide investment success standards, and GIPS requirements for Private Equity firms now. And I'll go through three or four of them because they're really useful metrics that you'll always come across, but they have drawbacks.

The Investment Multiple is the first of these factors. You can see the formula below.

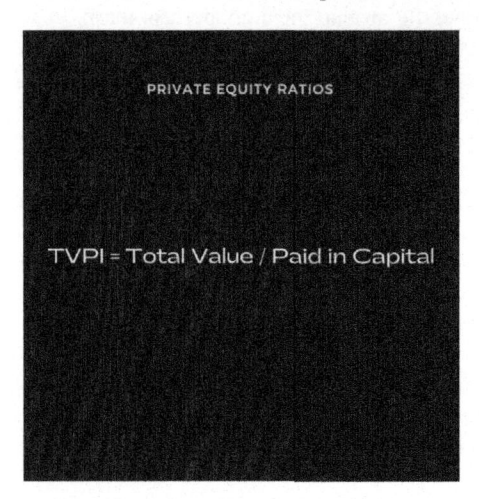

PRIVATE EQUITY RATIOS

TVPI = Total Value / Paid in Capital

Paid-in capital is linked to the magnitude of earnings and growth that may be expected. It's all about expectations, a big variable in determining stock prices. The TVPI is the total value of all issues divided by paid-in capital. The total money returned to the funds by the visit by the paid-in capital is divided among all capital sets, cumulative distributions, and residual value. This indicates the fund's total value compared to the initial capital invested in the fund. It's also important to remember that the charts show historical data, not future performance. Because of this, it may be difficult to determine if a particular investment is above or below its all-time high using these graphs. However, they provide a helpful comparison since they compare the prior year with the prior years. However, the time value of money is a problem.

The Second multiple is "The Realization Multiple," also known as DPI—distributions divided by Paid-in capital, so cumulative distributions are divided by Paid-in Capital.

PRIVATE EQUITY RATIOS

DPI = Distributions / Paid in Capital

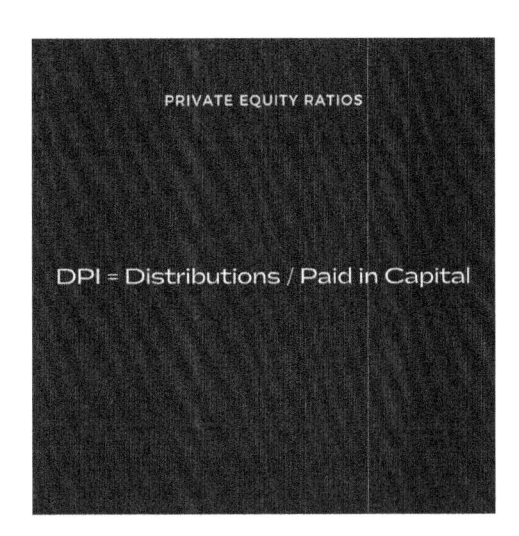

When compared with the fund's return, potential investors can determine how much of the fund's return has been paid out or realized rather than the return that has not. They've exited, and it's still theoretical. The residual value to be paid in capital multiple is the RV. I have all this information on the page because keeping track of everything is difficult.

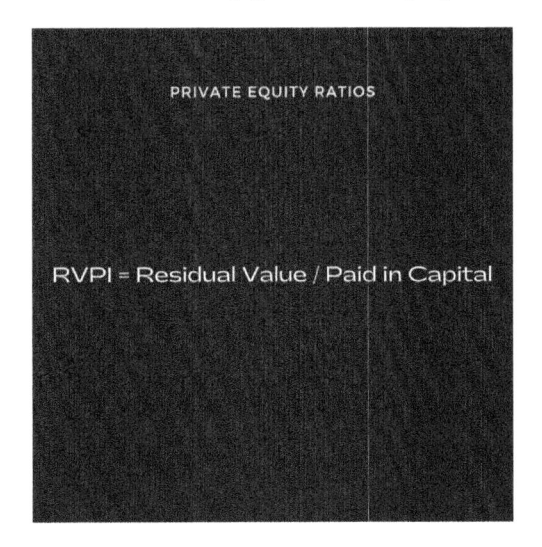

PRIVATE EQUITY RATIOS

RVPI = Residual Value / Paid in Capital

The Residual Value is the amount left over after paying out investors' cash gains. The RV is defined as the current market value of investments in the fund divided by payback or capital, and it's calculated as a percentage (%). The residual value is divided by the cash paid into the fund, which includes fees and other expenses incurred by Limited Partners.

The Internal Rate of Return (IRR) is a relatively simple concept, but knowing what the IRR is is good. And I'm not going into excruciating detail about the IRR here. Still, it's essentially the internal rate of return on a fund since its first investment. It's also crucial to evaluate it from the beginning. The Limited Partners have agreed to contribute money, and the investors have committed their capital. There may be a long period of time before they make their first investment. And you need to account for the IRR from the date of that initial investment. This measure takes into account the time value of money. This is why it's so critical. However, it also implies that you must know when things are happening since this can make a significant difference.

The Public Market Equivalent (PME) standard the SEC uses to compare fund performance to that of a corporation in an index such as the S&P 500 (double check name). So you're asking whether this fund has outperformed a prominent public company index like the S&P 500. Remember that several variant methods for calculating public market equivalents have been improving this statistic over the last 25 years. So, as with any of these things, the more you look at it, the more complex it becomes.

Taking it at face value, how does the fund compare to the public companies index in terms of performance? So, if you invested your money in the S&P 500, would you have done better or worse? Now, ratios are simple to compute and widely utilized, which is a useful statistic on the surface. When calculating fund performance. However, they do not consider the time value of money, which the IRR reflects.

The IRR isn't a ratio in this case. So, if you calculate a TVPI return over five years, would it be acceptable, good, or excellent three times? If it was over five years old, it might be. It would be less so if it were more than ten years old. But you have the same proportion. You want the total value to equal 100%. So you don't see the time value of money in that ratio. You see a simple proportion of the overall value and paid-in capital. When you have completed all of your investments and returned all funds to Limited Partners, you must keep in mind that these measures are only temporary. They may vary. The residual value might have a significant influence on it since residual value valuations are not simple. The residual values of these funds can be volatile, and the performance of the underlying companies may alter those values. A high initial residual value may underestimate the fund's value in the present moment. If it's high, it might overstate the fund's value. Still, you only learn whether residual values are correct after selling your position. You must understand what they represent and how to measure them. However, take another granular step and learn more about them. You'll discover that they're not as straightforward as they appear. That is just another reason why it's so compelling.

Section 17: Summary and Wrap-Up!

71. Time to wrap up the Book and Summarize It.

Now, it's time to wrap up the book and summarize it. First and foremost, congrats on finishing the book; it's a significant accomplishment. I hope you enjoyed it, learned much from it, and broadened your understanding of Private Equity.

Before signing off, let's briefly examine what we've covered so far. We began with a general overview of Private Equity. By looking at examples, get a sense of what Private Equity is all about. Then we spoke about how Private Equity funds work. Because terminology is so complex, I reviewed a dictionary of terms with you. Then, we talked about the most important aspects of Private Equity firms. If you're an entrepreneur, how can you discover your company's ideal Private Equity firm? That's a critical question, so I made sure we addressed it. Then, we looked at how Private Equity firms go about finding deals. Of course, we need to understand how Private Equity deals are structured, so we looked at deal value creation and KPIs before going through a step-by-step walkthrough of a Private Equity deal.

I dedicated a whole section to outlining due diligence in great depth because it is such a crucial element of the deal process. Of course, we needed to look at Private Equity valuation and pricing and understand the critical EBITDA measure. Of course, you were made aware of the rewards and risks associated with Private Equity, and we then addressed the options available, as you will need to exit the investment at some point.

We also covered recapitalizations while keeping the exits scenario in mind; we looked at sales through an M&A transaction and discussed IPOs, a typical way for PE firms to exit their investment portfolio companies. We must be mindful of the disadvantages. And I wanted to go through some reasons startups fail with you. After completing the procedure, we discussed calculating the returns to Private Equity investors, General Partners, and Limited Partners. In a nutshell, that was the book.

Please consider leaving an acceptable rating and review if you haven't already. Scan the QR code and it will take you directly to the review section of "Private Equity Finance Made Easy" on Amazon.com or you could visit the link mentioned below.

https://tinyurl.com/private-equity-review

In addition, I am available to answer any questions you may have regarding Private Equity. Write to me directly (mailto:umran@onecallbusinesssolutions.com). I'm always available to answer your inquiries and make every effort to do so as promptly as possible. That concludes the book's summary and conclusion. I hope you found it entertaining. I hope that was useful to you. I had a lot of fun putting it together for you. And I'm looking forward to connecting with you in another one of my titles.

72. Corporate Finance Further Learning

To further your learning within the Corporate Finance domain, I invite you to consider reading **"Mergers & Acquisitions Made Simple"** & **"The Venture Capital Playbook."** Each book serves as a specialization within the domain of your preference. Scan the QR codes or visit the links below to check out the books on Amazon.com.

https://tinyurl.com/mergers-made-simple | https://tinyurl.com/the-vc-playbook

I'd love to hear your thoughts on this book, write to me directly, mailto:umran@onecallbusinesssolutions.com.

PS *I personally respond to all of my emails. Feel free to write vicious troll-worthy mails. Everything goes. No filters!*

Cheers,
Umran Nayani

Printed in Great Britain
by Amazon